Trait Secrets

Winning together when
you DON'T think alike

By Judith A. Piani, CGA,
and Hedy Bookin-Weiner, Ph.D., CGA

Teric Publishing

Hollis, New Hampshire

Publisher's Cataloging-in-Publication Data
Piani, Judith A.
     Trait secrets : winning together when you don't think alike /
Judith A. Piani and Hedy Bookin-Weiner
vii, 168 p. : ill. ; 22 cm.
1. Personnel management. 2. Business. I. Title. II. Bookin-Weiner, Hedy
658.3'15-DDC21   00-104922
ISBN 0-9701272-0-0 (pbk.)   CIP

To Judi's son,
Todd Eric Piani
(October 31, 1968–August 18, 1995)

and Hedy's sister,
Deborah Bookin,
who became Todd's dearest friend

They showed us new possibilities and changed
us in ways we never could have imagined.
We will always be more grateful
than we could ever express.

Acknowledgments

From Judi

Many people have asked me to write a book on the trait system, but while I had a vision of what the book should be like and had made several attempts to write it over a number of years, I had never managed to get it on paper quite the way I envisioned it. After Hedy heard me speak at handwriting association meetings, she, too, asked me if there was a book available on the system. I told her there was a book, but it was still in my head.

A year later, after another meeting, Hedy asked me if the book was done. I told her that with my traits, I write as little as possible—so the book would take a long time. Hedy volunteered to help me write the book if I would, in exchange, teach her the trait system. Both of those goals have been met, and Hedy has now joined me in the business. She has been a joy to work with and has become a cherished friend.

We could not have accomplished this together without the support and assistance of many wonderful individuals. Some very special people helped me to refine the trait system in the early years. These were my early students, employees, co-consultants, and friends: Amanda Brauman, Pat Carter, Bob Ellis, Pearl Feeney-Grater, Fonda Monroe, and the late Theone Morgan. I have listed them alphabetically, and not in order of importance, as each has been important and dear to me.

Over the years, many clients have helped to broaden the application of the trait system. Among them are Gregg Anderson, Bob Bennett, Peter Brine, Sumner Burg, Art and Sharon Currier, Martin Hensel, Dave Ingemie, Dick Jondl, Jane Lundquist, Dr. Joe Marshall, Don McGuiness, Bill McLean, Steve Mesthos, Shelley Newman, Barbara Piette, Steve Ransom, Beverly Robsham, Ken White, Dr. Peter Williams, and others too numerous to mention.

Many, many friends have voiced their encouragement and listened patiently over the years. These include Joann and Bob Dellovo, Tom and Karen Lynch, Joe Meagher and Karen Peterson, Bob and Andy Morris, Laurea and Jim Nugent, Gail and Bob Quagan, Mimi Quinlan, Kate Pell, Christine Perez, Judie and Dave Stuart, Joyce Znamierowski, and my entire Monday-night group.

My dear friend Neil MacKenna has been my greatest source of encouragement almost from the beginning of my business career. His faith in me and in the work I do—and his continual prodding and support—have kept me going through good times and bad.

My loving husband, Brian Piani, has been an unending source of encouragement. His belief in me has sustained me through the years as well as through this project. My kids—Todd, Paige, Tobi, Kassi, Angela, Donna, and Jill—have lovingly shared their mom with this project. They were also my earliest source of information on traits and how to deal with them.

From Hedy

I am lucky to have many supportive and generous friends who have encouraged me over the years. They include Nancy Atkind, Barbara Caust, Jane Deutsch, Howard Friedman, Andrea Gingrande, Lynn Hallen, Linda Holland, Mickey Khazam, Sherry Leibowitz, Wendy Liebow, Tim Olcott, Judy Pappo, Toby Klang Ward, and Nancy Winsten. A number of friends who are authors themselves also provided empathy and helpful suggestions. I am grateful to Arthur Gingrande, Florence Harris, David Lukoff, Grant McLean, and Kay Kaufman Shelemay for their caring and expert advice. My dear friend Walter B. Miller, a wonderful writer who encourages and supports me in everything I do, helped with suggestions and editing. He also singlehandedly kept my computer (and me) from breaking down.

Although working on a book can have its difficult moments, what was most helpful was that I was working with Judi, so that even those difficult times had their delights. Our friendship and collaboration are proof that people with opposite traits can not only get along but truly thrive together and achieve more than either could alone.

Most important, I have had the support of a wonderful family. My loving parents, Robert and Lillian Bookin, have always been unbelievably supportive and encouraging. My sister, Deborah Bookin, who helped to edit the book, has been an almost daily source of inspiration and support. My daughter, Sara, has been a constant and loving cheerleader. Her witty and warm outlook and her belief in me always lift my spirits. My husband, Jerry Bookin-Weiner, has not only been a loving and supportive husband in all sorts of ways, but also went beyond the call of duty in reading, editing, and making suggestions on almost the entire manuscript.

From Both Judi and Hedy

It has been delightful working with Sharon Smith, our main editor and friend, who has been a font of knowledge about book production and has also made the book more enjoyable to read. She has been an unending supporter of this project as well as a source of encouragement.

We are grateful to Jean Achille, who jumped in at the end to teach us some ground rules of publishing and promotion. Even before she saw the manuscript, she added her support to the project, based solely on her faith in us.

We also thank Lida Stinchfield for her meticulous copyediting and for the encouraging support she offered even before she knew she would be working on this book.

Thanks to Dave Nelson, who created the wonderful illustrations that appear throughout the book and who designed both the cover and the text to make the book look as great as it does.

If we have left anyone out, it is not by design but by oversight. Please forgive us and know that your contributions are greatly appreciated.

Contents

Introduction

The Power of Awareness

What you don't know can hurt you

WE ONCE HEARD A NEWS REPORT ABOUT a police chief who came upon a motor-scooter accident almost immediately after it had occurred. An eight-year-old girl was bloodied but not seriously injured. Her father, however, was in far worse shape—unconscious and not breathing. Fortunately the chief knew what to do and had the necessary equipment. He immediately tried to insert a tube down the father's throat to allow him to breathe—at which point the child, thinking he was trying to hurt her father, tried to pull him away.

What the child didn't know could have delayed necessary action, denied her father the help he needed, and ultimately hurt the child herself (in this case, by costing the child her father). That sounds like the situation in a few offices we've seen! Well, maybe without the blood. . . It's true that the individuals in an office setting are typically older, but the misunderstandings and possibilities for unwanted repercussions are certainly there. And so is the assumption that the other person involved in a particular situation is acting out of malice or sheer craziness. Like the child at the accident scene, many people look at the actions in an office, find those actions totally alien to their own frames of reference, and infer all sorts of negative intentions on the part of others. If the people reaching those conclusions knew more of the story, lots of grief could be avoided. And that is why we wrote this book.

The modern office, as all those legions of Dilbert fans will gleefully attest, often seems a wild and crazy place. How can the boss be so unreasonable, the subordinates so uncooperative, the whole place so incredibly unproductive? Well, maybe all is not quite what it seems. There is order, and reason, and even good intentions under much of the apparent madness. Really. Once you understand what's actually going on, you can accomplish things you never dreamed possible. It's understanding that gives you power.

Do you remember the old story of the blind men and the elephant? The first blind man felt the elephant's side, and said, "Oh, an elephant is like a large wall!" The second blind man felt the elephant's tusk and said, "Oh, an elephant is like a sharp spear!" The third blind man felt the elephant's trunk and said, "Oh, an elephant is like a giant snake!" And so it went, with each blind man touching a different part of the elephant and each reaching a totally different conclusion about what the animal looked like. Each was absolutely correct about his own experience—but literally in the dark about what the others were concluding. And none of them had a clue how all those pieces—the side, the tusk, the trunk—fit together to form the complete picture, the elephant.

So it often is in business. We usually see what we expect to see, and—like the blind men and the elephant—we see things in ways

And so it went, with each blind man touching a different part of the elephant and each reaching a totally different conclusion about what the animal looked like.

that are limited by our own experience and perceptions. The goal of this book is to help you recognize how others may be looking at the exact same situations you're seeing—and viewing them in ways that may never have occurred to you.

When Judi Piani started working with businesses more than 20 years ago, she noticed how certain behaviors were causing problems in the workplace, but she saw those behaviors in a totally new and different way. Judi saw automatic, instinctive reactions (traits) that had a powerful influence on the operations of every company she dealt with, even though the traits weren't consciously noticed or discussed. What did get discussed were some of the behaviors caused by the traits—usually described by terms like "stupid" or "mean" or just plain "crazy."

Judi recognized that although the traits themselves were not inherently good or bad, the behavior they caused could result in great difficulties, depending on the situation or context in which they were displayed. Someone who has a hard time figuring out what to do next is not by definition a morally inferior person, but you wouldn't put that person in charge of an air-traffic-control tower. Perceptions could make certain behaviors—and even certain individuals—seem good or bad when people did not understand the motivation or reasoning behind the behavior. And this meant that an understanding of traits could make a world of difference in the workplace.

Someone who has a hard time figuring out what to do next is not by definition a morally inferior person, but you wouldn't put that person in charge of an air-traffic-control tower.

Judi wanted to talk to her clients about the traits she had identified, but there were no names for these patterns of instinctive, automatic behavior. So she developed her own, creating a special vocabulary to describe the traits. That's when the Piani Trait System was born.

The Piani Trait System consists of the 25 traits Judi identified as affecting the work environment most significantly. They are the keys to understanding what is happening on both the individual and organizational levels. A crucial aspect of the Piani Trait System is that none of these traits is judged good or bad. Rather, each is advantageous or disadvantageous, depending upon the circumstances. In this book we discuss ten of these traits that have an enormous overall impact and cause numerous misunderstandings.

After seeing how helpful the Piani Trait System had proven to be in the office, many clients brought in their spouses and children to benefit from it. Some of their stories are in this book, with names, occupations, and sometimes genders changed—as they have been in the other stories we've included—for privacy. These clients found the system equally helpful in promoting more positive and productive relationships at home, and for years they have been asking for a book on it. This is our response to those requests.

What This Book Will Do for You

This book will help you to develop a kind of X-ray vision into people and organizations that will allow you to achieve your objectives. You can learn how to:

- understand why people are behaving in a certain way and figure out how to respond to their behavior
- find the people who can help you succeed personally and organizationally
- deal more effectively with people who seem difficult
- anticipate the direction in which your company can or will or should be going

The Piani Trait System gives you the tools to understand where people are coming from and why they act the way they do. It helps you find productive responses to people's behavior, rather than dwelling on what you assume to be their personalities or motivations. You will learn specific techniques for working with people whose traits clash with yours, the ones that usually cause the most misunderstandings. These techniques will help you to avert conflict in both your personal and your professional relationships.

The Piani Trait System will also help you to reassess how you come across to others. Once you become aware of your own traits and understand them in a nonjudgmental way, you can make decisions about whether your instinctive behavior is appropriate in dealing with specific people or situations. Awareness of instinctive responses can give you incredible power to change your behavior and inform your choices.

How We Find Traits

Once you are aware of the traits, you will recognize them in the people around you—and in yourself. It is the awareness of these traits that will reveal a new world of meaning to you. However, as consultants, we don't have a lot of time to observe, so we use handwriting analysis as a quick, accurate way to identify an individual's traits.

We know that not everyone will be comfortable with that approach. Despite the fact that corporations are increasingly recognizing handwriting analysis as an important tool for personality assessment in hiring and team building, we are aware that some people may be dubious about its validity as a tool for identifying personality traits.

In the end, that doesn't really matter. Whether you believe in handwriting analysis or not, it's the traits themselves that are important here, and you don't need to know handwriting analysis to recognize them. But for the benefit of those who have wanted to know how we identify the traits through handwriting, we have included at the end of each chapter a description (and illustration) of a major handwriting indicator for each trait discussed. That way, if you are uncertain about the cause of the behavior you see and think that it might be a particular trait, you can check for the indicator in the handwriting to confirm—or contradict—your understanding.

A word of caution here: Analyzing handwriting is a complex endeavor. Every indicator in handwriting has to be considered in the context of the writing as a whole; otherwise you risk becoming just one more blind man examining the elephant. This book is not intended to make you an expert at interpreting handwriting. It is intended to give you a clear understanding of traits.

In short, handwriting analysis is a quick way to get at the traits when you don't have the time to hang around and observe a situation, but once you are aware of the traits, you will see them everywhere. And they will change the way you understand the world.

A New Perspective on You

An understanding of traits can be rewarding in another way, too: Not only will it guide you in your relationships with others, but it can also help you appreciate yourself more. As you will discover in the following chapters, people often judge themselves or others negatively when in fact they are simply in the wrong situations for their traits. Even someone who is highly successful will be stressed and may never realize his full potential if his traits aren't right for the situation.

We know of a company in which one executive, Mark, had consistently outperformed his colleagues. He was so successful that when it came time to select a new president, he was offered the job—but he turned it down, wanting to remain where he was. After the new president, Aaron, came on the job, he evaluated the whole company for a year. Then he fired Mark.

You can imagine how incensed Mark was! Yet a year later he was mentally thanking Aaron for firing him. Mark had gone into consulting instead of administration, and was happier than he had ever been in his life. In retrospect, Mark saw the toll taken by the stress of a job that did not fit his traits well. When your traits don't match your position, it takes a lot more effort to make things work, and he had been putting in an extraordinary amount of time and energy. By dint of Mark's sheer brilliance and effort, he still had managed to be very successful. But when he went into a consulting job that better fit his traits, he was not only outstandingly successful, but was also much happier and wealthier, with less effort.

Sounds pretty good, doesn't it? But can you make a change or improve your current situation just as successfully? You bet. Everyone has special talents that can shine if placed in the right environment. The keys are to identify those talents (or traits) and the environment in which they can flourish. And that, in combination with recognizing the traits of others, is what this book is all about.

Chapter One

"Normal Is What I Am"

So what's the matter with *them*?

MOST PEOPLE THINK "NORMAL" behavior is whatever behavior comes naturally *to them*. You hear it all the time, when someone says, "Wouldn't anyone do that in a crisis?" or "Wouldn't anyone react the same way?" or "Wouldn't anyone want that for their kids?" Intellectually, we know that everyone is different, but in our guts, each of us thinks that normal people behave exactly the same way we do. In other words, while we might not always be ready to acknowledge it, each of us instinctively believes one thing:

"Normal Is What I Am."

Take Lillian, a hands-on manager who was intimately involved in every detail of her subordinates' work. She often went in and helped her subordinates actually execute their projects, and when she wasn't helping, she expected them to report to her often about how things were going, so she could review their progress.

Then there was Donna, a hands-off manager who would go around and briefly ask each of her subordinates how things were going. Donna never actually got involved in doing the work with them. She advised, but she didn't participate in the implementation of assignments.

Lillian viewed Donna as not managing correctly. She thought Donna was lazy, uncommitted, careless, and guilty of delegating far too much. Donna thought Lillian was a control freak who stifled her employees.

Each believed that her behavior was the normal and right way to supervise—"Normal is what I am." And because the other person was behaving differently, each assumed that the other was not a good, concerned manager. They judged each other negatively, which put a strain on their working relationship.

Why Do People Behave in Such Different Ways?

We all know that people have different values and different belief systems, but even those who profess to have similar values and beliefs may behave quite differently. Mickey and Lynn, for example, shared at least one value in which both believed strongly: making good use of time. However, when given an assignment for an ad campaign that was due in a month, their approaches were very different. Mickey started on the campaign immediately and worked on it a few hours every day, along with her other responsibilities. Lynn didn't look at the file until the week before it was due, then worked on it nonstop, skipping lunch and staying late. Both turned in their work on time. However, Mickey watched Lynn working late and thought, "She doesn't manage her time well. She wouldn't be plowing through like this if she had started on time. She procrastinates, she's disorganized, and she does a rush job."

Lynn, during the week before the campaign was due, noticed Mickey going to lunch, taking coffee breaks, and leaving on time. Her conclusion? "Mickey's uncommitted. She's wasting time with lunch and coffee breaks. She'll turn in a superficial job." Each felt that she was spending more time and energy than the other on the project.

Both Lynn and Mickey wanted to use time effectively and wisely. So why were their behaviors so different? Was it different motivation? Was Lynn's motivation to avoid a disliked task by procrastinating? Was Mickey's motivation to avoid giving the project her all?

The Banker and the Robber

Our experience has led us to believe that most people want to be as successful as possible while acting according to their own values and beliefs. A banker wants to do the best job possible in running the bank, so the bank's business and profits will increase. The bank robber wants to do the best job possible at robbing the bank so he will get a lot of money without getting caught. Their values are very different, but both have the same motivation: to do the best job they can.

How many people get up in the morning saying, "I want to do the worst job possible, be a pain in the neck, and fail at everything"? Both Lynn and Mickey had the same motivation: to do the best job they could and be as successful as possible. It was not their values or their beliefs that caused their different behavior, because they had the same values and beliefs. So how could they act so differently?

Trait Secrets

The answer is simple. While both Mickey and Lynn felt it was important to use time efficiently, each used different automatic and instinctive behaviors to achieve that shared value. These instinctive patterns of behavior result from "traits." However, these are not the traits you hear about in everyday conversation.

What Is a Trait?

We all accept the fact that we are born with different physical traits: eye color, skin color, height, body shape, etc. We may like or dislike our traits, but, short of undergoing major surgery, we can't change them. The irony is that different societies value these traits differently. Today's ads extol a slim female body as a beautiful thing, but the paintings of 17th-century artists like Rubens reflect very different values. In that period, a considerably more robust female form was considered both voluptuous and beautiful. Similarly, in certain modern cultures, it's considered a compliment when someone says you look as though you have gained weight. (Wouldn't we all like to live in those cultures?)

Traits are not intrinsically good or bad, attractive or unattractive. They are merely descriptions that allow people to recognize us. If we say someone has brown eyes, an image comes to mind, while blue eyes evoke a different image. Brown eyes are not better or worse than blue eyes—just different.

Recognizing Behavioral Traits

Societies have given names to physical traits so that they are generally recognized and understood. Societies have also given names to personality traits—things like "soft spoken," "hot tempered," and "tactful." But unlike the descriptions of physical traits, these personality descriptions do not mean the same thing to everyone who hears them. If an individual is described as being "hot tempered," one person might have an image of someone punching a wall or throwing dishes. Another might envision someone who gets red faced and rushes from the room. The descriptive phrase is the same, yet the images that come to mind are different. This doesn't occur when we say "brown eyes." We all have the same image of brown eyes.

What Comes to Mind?

When we try to describe people's behavior, the words used in everyday conversation can suggest very different things to different people. But what if we knew that when we said "hot tempered," certain specific behaviors would occur—say, breaking crockery and screaming at a certain number of decibels? Then we would know what to expect and could prepare to deal with the behavior in appropriate ways—perhaps buying earplugs or finding a broom.

This is where the Piani Trait System comes into play. Rather than working with the old words, with their wide ranges of interpretation, the Piani Trait System assigns a specific meaning to each trait name. When someone uses a trait name, everyone knows what behaviors to associate with that trait. The image in everyone's mind is consistent.

The image is also very meaningful. The traits described in this book have been found crucial to the success or failure of individuals, relationships, and organizations. Yet these traits do not imply value judgments. Like brown eyes or blue eyes, one is not better than the other. So why do they sometimes cause problems?

Choosing Hammers and Saws

Your traits are like tools; a specific one may be more or less helpful in a particular environment. When you think of having a particular trait, think of having a hammer or having a saw. You can't say that one of the tools is better than the other; it really depends on what you want to do. If you want to drive a nail into wood, the hammer is better. When you want to cut a piece of wood, the saw is better. Like a tool, a specific trait may be more or less helpful in

***Like a tool, a specific trait may be more or less helpful in a
particular situation.***

a particular situation.

Our personality traits are not something we can choose, any more
than we can choose the brown eyes or blue eyes we're born with.
We just need to make the best use of what we have. (There is always
some discussion about whether traits are determined by environ-
mental or hereditary factors. We think both play a role. In this book,
however, what we are concerned with is not how we got our traits,
but rather how they influence our behavior.) As with our physical
traits, we can either accept our personality traits or go to a lot of
trouble—therapy, say, or a lobotomy—to try to change them.

Mickey and Lynn had opposite traits. Mickey had the Non-
Pressure trait, while Lynn had the Pressure trait. People with the
Non-Pressure trait do their best and most creative work if they can
pace themselves, starting well in advance and taking breaks. Anyone
with the Non-Pressure trait would behave in a similar fashion.

Those with the Pressure trait, on the other hand, do their best
work under the gun at the last minute, in one fell swoop. Taking
breaks distracts them, and pressure spurs their creativity. Any person
with the Pressure trait would work much the way Lynn did.

Mickey and Lynn each knew how she produced her own best work and thought that was the only way anyone could produce good work. "Normal is what I am," the reasoning goes, "so if you are behaving differently from the way I behave, you are not trying to do your best."

If You Want to Nail It, You Can't Use a Saw

In this case, both traits could produce good work, albeit through different behaviors. However, in some cases, certain traits cannot produce the best result. Just as a saw is not the best tool to pound a nail, a particular trait is not always helpful in every situation. The trait itself is not good or bad; it is just more or less helpful in a particular circumstance.

If Mickey, who doesn't do her best work under pressure, had wanted to be a firefighter, she would have had difficulty fighting fires for hours on end. If Mickey had really wanted to be in firefighting, she would have been better suited to an administrative job at a fire station, one that would allow her to pace herself and not be driven by pressured circumstances.

Lynn, on the other hand, would have found an administrative job unbearably boring. With no pressure to drive her, she would have had a hard time producing good work. Lynn would have been in her element with the intensity and pressure of fighting fires for hours on end.

Perceptions Are Everything

Lynn's perception of Mickey was derived from the fact that Lynn herself did her best work under pressure, so she believed that anyone who did not work that way was not trying to do her best. She made negative judgments about Mickey's motivation and values, concluding that Mickey was lazy and didn't value good work or efficiency. Mickey had similar misperceptions about Lynn, based on Mickey's own traits. She thought waiting until the last minute indicated lack of motivation—or that it was a sign of disorganization and procrastination. Neither noticed that the other produced fine work; they were too focused on the behavior to pay attention to the result.

Cooking with Traits

Individuals have different combinations of traits that make them as unique as their fingerprints. That's why many typologies in business and self-help industries don't always work. A type contains a certain group of traits, but not everyone assigned to the type has all the traits—and in fact, some people sharing a type may have some very opposite traits. That is why we present each trait or pair of traits separately.

If you've ever done any cooking, you know that three people could follow the same eight-ingredient recipe, but if one adds extra salt, another leaves out the salt, and the third puts in the correct amount, their creations will taste different. Despite the fact that the first seven ingredients were exactly the same, changing the amount of the eighth ingredient will significantly change the

If two chefs start to cook using flour, but each then adds different ingredients to the mix, they could end up with products as diverse as cake and pasta.

taste of the finished product. Similarly, three people can have the same trait, but if the degree to which each possesses it is different, each will behave differently.

And think what will happen if the other ingredients in the recipe are not the same. If all three people start to cook using flour, but each then adds different ingredients to the mix, they could end up with products as diverse as cake, pasta, and papier-mâché. By the same token, if three individuals share one trait, but differ on a number of others, they may appear to be quite different—so much so that it might be hard to believe they have *any* traits in common. Differences in the traits we possess and the degrees to which we possess them cause our personalities to be as individual as our fingerprints. And that's what makes life interesting. *Frustrating* sometimes, but interesting nevertheless.

Most typologies include many traits within one type; they break the personality puzzle into large pieces. Someone who for the most part seems to fit a particular type will not have all the traits generally associated with that type. In fact, she is likely to have other traits not included in the type—some of which can add significant "flavor" to her personality. The Piani Trait System breaks things into smaller, more meaningful pieces, letting you customize the identification of traits and put together a "type" that is unique for each individual. And it allows you to do it without giving a half-hour test to a test-savvy person. (The quizzes included in this book are intended to help you quickly determine which traits you have. Sure, you could "beat the system" and give answers that would indicate certain traits—but since the traits aren't good or bad, what would be the point?)

What Flavor Is a Company?

Just as a unique combination and intensity of particular traits contributes to individuality in people, so the traits of an executive team combine to create a unique culture within each organization.

Everyone knows that different companies have different cultures. By identifying the traits of the executive team, we can identify the culture of an organization and see if that culture provides the best tools to meet the company goals. And if it doesn't, we can figure out ways to adjust it.

One company that was losing market share decided to replace its CEO—but chose as its new chief executive someone who had the same traits as the old one. Since "normal is what I am," and the board of directors was operating without an awareness of traits, the directors instinctively selected a new CEO with traits similar to their own. And they continued getting similar results: more loss of market share. The company actually needed a CEO with traits exactly the opposite of the ones their successive CEOs had, but since the company didn't recognize the role of traits, the death spiral continued.

Reduce Your Stress, Increase Your Success

An understanding of traits gives you a more comprehensive view of how and why others behave the way they do—and more choices as you determine how to reach your own goals. It can also reduce your stress level as you recognize that many of the behaviors that irritated you in the past are not the result of incompetence, malice, or sheer lunacy. Rather, an understanding of traits will allow you to see people as trying to do their best, but in ways you would never have dreamed possible.

Once you understand your own traits and how they relate to those of others, you will realize how others may have been perceiving *your* actions, too—and how you might be able to correct any misperceptions. And it gets better! A knowledge of traits empowers you to deal with others more effectively and to achieve your goals. It can help you to:
- increase productivity
- reach agreements that hold

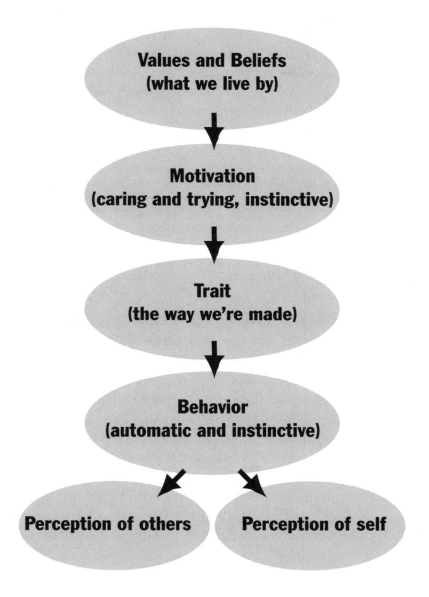

Even when people share very similar values, beliefs, and motivations, their traits can cause them to behave differently.

- deal with producers of red tape
- match the corporate culture to the goals of the company
- determine if your traits are a good match for the corporate culture
- achieve better relationships, both personally and professionally
- determine whom you need to work with to make your traits more effective
- place yourself and others in situations in which you'll be most successful.

Isn't a little power, gained through understanding, a wonderful thing?

In Short

The most critical elements of the Piani Trait System can be summarized in a few key points.

- We all share the same motivation: to try to be as successful as we can while acting according to our values and beliefs.
- Our traits are the tools we are given or the way we are made.
- Our behaviors are our automatic and instinctive responses, resulting from those traits.
- The perceptions we have of others result from our interpretation of their behavior through our trait filters.
- The perceptions others have of us result from their interpretation of our behavior through their own trait filters.

Chapter Two

Pressure and Non-Pressure

When it only *looks* like procrastination

THE PROJECT IS DUE ON THE FIFTEENTH. Joe begins working on it as soon as he gets the assignment, and he gets something done on it every day. He finishes by the 12th. Ann gets the project at the same time but doesn't have time to work on it until the 12th. From that point on, she spends almost all her time on the project, completing it after an all-nighter on the 14th. Her work is just as good as Joe's.

Pressure and Non-Pressure
Who Are You?

After each question, circle the answer
that comes closest to describing you.

1. I feel I do a better job when I have more than enough lead time on a project.
a) Usually
b) It depends
c) Not really

2. In a crisis, I rise to the occasion. I often impress myself, and sometimes even others, with how well I perform.
a) Rarely
b) Sometimes
c) Usually

3. Given a choice between a job in which the workload is pretty steady and one in which I often need to deal with crises, I prefer
a) a job in which the pace is even.
b) a job in between the two extremes.
c) a job with some excitement—give me a crisis over boredom any day!

4. I skip one or more meals a day when I'm engrossed in a project.
a) Never
b) Occasionally
c) Frequently. Who needs food when a deadline's looming?

5. Others often accuse me of procrastinating. My response is that

a) I try not to procrastinate. I know that when I do put things off, I finish late.
b) I sometimes put things off until the last minute, but most of the time I still finish by the deadline.
c) I do put things off as long as possible, but I seldom miss a deadline.

6. If I were in high school or college, I would cram for exams and do projects or papers at the last minute.
a) Rarely or never
b) Occasionally
c) Usually

7. If I skip lunch, I get a headache or generally don't feel my best.
a) Usually
b) Sometimes
c) Lunch? What's lunch?

8. If the deadline for a short project were a month away, but I had the time to work on it now, I would
a) get to work and pace myself, working on it throughout the month.
b) wait until the last minute, then focus all my energy on it.
c) either pace myself or wait, depending on the situation.

Have you ever wondered why some people seem to be confronted by so many crises and why they always have to work up to the last minute? Perhaps instead you have puzzled over how people can ever manage to finish ahead of time. The answer may be found in an understanding of the Pressure and the Non-Pressure traits.

Can the Tortoise and the Hare Ever Understand Each Other?

Joe has the Non-Pressure trait. Ann has the Pressure trait. They probably don't even know this. Like all traits, these operate unconsciously and automatically. All Ann and Joe may know is that, to each of them, the other's work pattern seems bizarre—to put it politely. Individuals possess the Pressure or Non-Pressure trait, like all traits, to varying degrees along a continuum, and people at either extreme of the continuum find it difficult to understand how or why those at the opposite extreme can function the way they do.

9. When I'm in the middle of a project,
a) I like to stick with it until I'm done.
b) I take frequent breaks—need that doughnut!
c) the number of breaks I take depends on how I feel.

10. I do my best work under a tight deadline.
a) Never—that's definitely not me!
b) Sometimes
c) Always—pressure is my motivator!

SCORING
Add up your total score, using the following values for your answers.

1.	a) 0	b) 2	c) 5
2.	a) 0	b) 3	c) 5
3.	a) 0	b) 3	c) 5
4.	a) 0	b) 3	c) 5
5.	a) 0	b) 3	c) 5
6.	a) 0	b) 2	c) 5
7.	a) 0	b) 2	c) 5
8.	a) 0	b) 5	c) 3
9.	a) 5	b) 0	c) 3
10.	a) 0	b) 3	c) 5

A score between 0 and 15 indicates a Non-Pressure trait. Anything from 16 through 30 shows a moderate Pressure trait, and a score higher than 30 means a strong Pressure trait.

The Pressure Trait: Normal Time, Uptime, and Downtime

People with the Pressure trait have three modes of operation. They're either in normal time, when they perform to average levels; in uptime, when they perform to optimal levels; or in downtime, when they're barely working at all.

Normal Time

Few organizations function under constant crises. During normal time there are no current crises, problems, or deadlines. During normal time, people with the Pressure trait work only to about average levels for their capabilities. They may go to lunch, take coffee breaks, and chat with coworkers, while working at a moderate level.

Uptime

However, given a crisis or a deadline, those with the Pressure trait have the ability to go into uptime. When they are in uptime, they are in high gear, on a roll, fully in-

Normal time

Uptime

The Pressure person thrives on crisis, accomplishes the task . . .

volved. They can accomplish more in two hours of uptime than in a whole day of normal time. The adrenaline rush enables them to get more done—and to do it better—during this period than at any other time.

Uptime feels good to a person with the Pressure trait. The adrenaline rush provides a kind of high. Pressure people in uptime become unaware of their bodies. If they are hungry or have colds, they don't think about that. They barely think about bodily needs at all.

They don't have time to think about trivial matters like lunch or health because they have bigger things on their minds. In uptime, the focus and creativity of the Pressure individual are at a peak. This person is functioning at her optimum level, and it feels wonderful. During this period the person with the Pressure trait likes to do things in one fell swoop. If she had to stop for lunch it would feel as if the momentum had been lost and she would have to gear up all over again. Her self-esteem increases as she realizes how well she is working and how much she is accomplishing.

This trait can cause people consciously or unconsciously to put off projects to precipitate the uptime mode that feels so great. This is not procrastination. Procrastinators put things off not because they love to work in uptime, but because they don't want to deal with the project—perhaps for fear of failure or for other reasons. When a procrastinator finally gets to a project, it's likely he won't enjoy it. The worker with the Pressure trait will. He could be cursing the situation that

Downtime

. . . then needs downtime.

caused the uptime, but uptime is actually his favorite work mode.

People who have the Pressure trait thrive on crises. Thus, the instinctive, normal behavior for anyone with the Pressure trait is to wait until she's under the gun. This is the college student who knows two months ahead of time when the term paper is due, but waits until three days before the deadline to start. She then works day and night, hands the paper in on time, and crashes. Sound familiar? The college student who crams for exams and does papers at the last minute is a classic example of someone with the Pressure trait. This student sometimes looks at the Non-Pressure students with envy, vowing to start earlier next semester. But she won't. Her automatic and instinctive behavior is to wait until the last minute to act. Had such a student finished earlier (and this does happen sometimes), she would have redone a lot of her work at the last minute, because that's when she is most creative.

Note that the Pressure student could get all A's or all C's—and so could the Non-Pressure student. Having the Pressure trait does not determine the quality of the end result, only the approach that will be taken to get there. Similarly, in a work environment the Pressure trait is not an indicator of how well a person will do a particular job, only the approach that will be used.

Downtime

Once the deadline is met, the individual with the Pressure trait crashes. The crashing is downtime. During downtime the body physically and emotionally replenishes what it used up in uptime mode. During downtime the individual becomes conscious of her body again—and of hunger, fatigue, and thirst.

After being in uptime mode all day long, still feeling great, the individual with the Pressure trait gets in the car to go home and suddenly feels like a balloon with a slow leak. Downtime is starting, and it can start within minutes of finishing uptime.

In downtime, someone with the Pressure trait feels like "vegging out" and doing nothing—except, perhaps, eating a horse, since those with the Pressure trait hardly eat at all during uptime. Downtime is the time for real relaxation—reading, watching television, puttering in the garden. We once had a client whose handwriting indicated that he was in burnout. Judi asked, "Do you ever get any downtime?"

"Sure," he replied. "Every Saturday I go skydiving."

This was downtime in a very literal sense, all right, but it wasn't the type of activity Judi meant. However enjoyable it may be, anything that gives you an adrenaline rush is not downtime.

It's important not to underestimate the role of downtime as an essential part of the cycle for the Pressure individual. It is during downtime that those with the Pressure trait replenish physically and emotionally. If the Pressure employee loses out on downtime because of constant crises at the office, and then comes home to more work or another crisis, there is no chance for downtime. Eventually, burnout results. Insufficient downtime is the source of much executive burnout.

Downtime is similar to scheduled maintenance on your car. Every 3,000 miles you're supposed to change the oil. You can be busy and go 5,000, 7,000, 10,000, or even 20,000 miles without changing the oil, but the car will start to run rough—and if you let it go long enough, you will do major damage to the car. The same principle applies to the human body. Skipping downtime for a person with the Pressure trait is like skipping oil changes for a car. Eventually the body, like the car, will run rough—and the stress will manifest itself in health problems like ulcers, high blood pressure, migraines, the flu, or a backache.

If the worker with the Pressure trait keeps pushing beyond this stage, continuing to ignore the need for downtime, the result can be extensive damage to the body—like a heart attack or stroke. This is not to say that all heart attacks come from lack of downtime, but lack of downtime is one source of stress—and medical research consistently cites stress as a major source of physical ills.

The day or two after a major project is completed within a corporation, employees often mill around without getting much done. The employees with the Pressure trait are really in downtime mode then. Corporations need to acknowledge this pattern in order to avoid executive and worker burnout. Some companies are known for burning out and spitting out their employees. People are never quite the same after they've burned out, and the more they keep pushing after they've entered burnout, the deeper they go into it and the longer it takes to come back—if they ever do.

The Owner's Guide to the Pressure Trait: Deadlines, Downtime, and Understanding

As hard as it is for those with the Non-Pressure trait to imagine, individuals with the Pressure trait actually *need* pressure to do their best work. They are less successful when they're not confronted with periodic deadlines. Without a deadline, there's no pressure. Without pressure, there's no adrenaline rush for the Pressure individual. And without the adrenaline rush, that person won't produce his best work. So if you have a strong Pressure trait, it's important that your work have some pressure in the form of deadlines. Your boss—or your clients, if you're self-employed—can set the deadlines. Or you can create the pressure yourself by determining your own deadlines. You might decide, "I've got a project due in two months. My goal is to finish by next week." And then you would go into uptime to do that. Whether you need to have that pressure come from within or from someone else depends on your other traits, but it's likely that you'll know instinctively which source is best for you. What's important is that you *have* deadlines. You'd be very unhappy as, say, a toll collector. You could also be a very discontented retiree. When people with the Pressure trait retire, they need to focus their attention on something new, and that something new—volunteer work, a second career, or college—needs to involve deadlines.

Pressure individuals thrive on uptime and do not want to give it up. When Hedy, who has the Non-Pressure trait, married Jerry, who has the Pressure trait, she discovered that it was typical for him to stay up all night writing a grant proposal that had to be postmarked the next day. She couldn't understand why he hadn't thought to start earlier and work a little each evening—and she pointed out this possibility to him. She told him that he needed his rest. But nothing worked, and she began to view him, her previously

People kept telling her what a dynamo he was at work, but at home he wanted to do nothing but veg out and watch television.

flawless husband, as a terrible procrastinator. Late one evening she said sarcastically, "I think you actually *like* doing things at the last minute!" To her surprise, he agreed. He said he loved the adrenaline rush and pointed out that he had never actually missed a deadline (although there had been some mighty close calls). He also had an enviable record of winning grants. Hedy realized that he wasn't disorganized or procrastinating; he enjoyed operating that way.

But Hedy was still mystified by something else about Jerry. People kept telling her what a dynamo he was at work, but at home he wanted to do nothing but veg out and watch television. It was like hearing about Superman in the workplace, then watching him change back into Clark Kent every evening at home. Then Hedy learned about the Pressure trait and downtime, and everything fell into place. The typical person with the Pressure trait needs at least one day a week of downtime, although he can take it as two half days or three evenings—Jerry's nights in front of the television. It's essential that anyone with a high Pressure trait find a way to get that downtime. It's also essential for that person to understand his opposite, the individual with the Non-Pressure trait.

The Non-Pressure Trait: Give Me a Break!

The Non-Pressure trait shows up in the college student who has a term paper due in two months and who starts today, works on it 45 minutes each day, and finishes two weeks before it's due. Yes, Pressure readers, such people really do exist. And they can't understand

The Non-Pressure person works steadily . . .

you, either. We tend to see slightly more of the Pressure trait among the executives who consult us, but we have seen many Non-Pressure individuals who are effective at all levels, including presidents. Both traits can work well at any level if they're complemented appropriately by the traits of the rest of the team.

An individual with the Non-Pressure trait is like a big car with a small gas tank. He runs at his optimal level consistently if he can take short intermittent refueling breaks throughout the day. As long as he fills up often, he can maintain his optimal working mode. So he may work two hours, then take a coffee break and relax for ten minutes or so. Then he'll work for another two hours and break for lunch. And so it goes.

It is good for this person to take in some food or drink during the break. It doesn't have to be a five-course meal, but eating or drinking some small amount literally refreshes a person with this trait, setting him up to continue the task at hand. Non-Pressure individuals need at least three, and sometimes as many as six, small meals a day in order to function at an optimal level. And that may

. . . and requires frequent breaks.

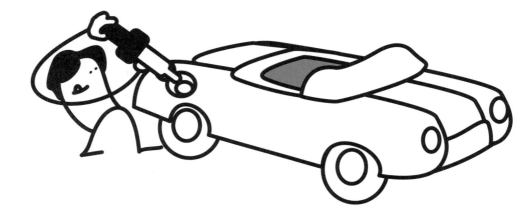

***An individual with the Non-Pressure trait is like a big car
with a small gas tank.***

be *in addition* to a few stops for coffee or juice. Some people have
to break every 45 minutes, some every hour and a half; the length
of time between breaks varies from one individual to the next.
What's consistent is the need for breaks of some sort. If those with
the Non-Pressure trait can't get breaks, they start to burn out, just
as those with the Pressure trait do when they can't get sufficient
downtime.

Lead Time: Only 364 Shopping Days 'Til Christmas

Individuals with the Non-Pressure trait like to have plenty of
lead time, to know the schedule well in advance so they can pace
themselves. The ones with the Non-Pressure trait are the ones who
start their Christmas shopping months in advance and do it a little at a time until they're done. The shoppers with the Pressure trait
are in the stores three days before Christmas. We all know Christmas is coming. . .

The Owner's Guide to the Non-Pressure Trait

If you have the Non-Pressure trait, you need to be sure to get your breaks. You can skip one occasionally, but if you do this a lot, your work will suffer. And *you* will suffer—with fatigue or with aches wherever your weak points are. And how do you make sure you don't miss too many of those essential breaks? Your mantra needs to become the same as that of the worker with the Pressure trait: "What matters isn't *how* I do it, but how *well* I do it."

Breaks will be less of an issue if your work is suited to your Non-Pressure trait. You need to be in a job where there are few last-minute crises—or if there *are* last-minute crises, you're not the one who's called upon to deal with them. You need a supervisor who understands the importance of lead time. If you are in sales, you need yearly quotas, not weekly ones. You need a job in which you have the freedom to pace yourself.

Mind Over Matter Can Be the Matter

While it's characteristic of someone with the Non-Pressure trait to need breaks, the person with the Pressure trait can reach a point at which he needs breaks, too. But for the one with the Pressure trait, that need is symptomatic of burnout. If you have the Pressure trait and have burned out, you may not realize that your body is now behaving like that of a Non-Pressure person, while your mind still wants to function as that of someone with the Pressure trait. Be careful. Your mind can force your body into further burnout if you don't take those breaks. Even if you don't feel like it. Even if you need to keep going for only another three hours to finish the project. Even if your supervisor thinks you're a wimp. (Show your Pressure boss this chapter.)

What If You Don't Fit Either Trait?

Then there are those people who have some characteristics of both traits. Most of the time they work in the paced mode, but when pressure is applied, they can go into uptime. For these people, however, uptime mode is shorter than for those who have the extreme Pressure trait. Some Pressure workers can stay in uptime for 24 hours. Others—particularly those who are midway along the continuum between Pressure and Non-Pressure—can stay in uptime for only five hours before they must stop and eat. And while they may be able to rise to the occasion when a deadline looms, they wouldn't really want to work that way on a regular basis. It's only the worker with the true Pressure trait who actually *thrives* in uptime and crisis.

Some people who look like procrastinators are really Pressure individuals who, knowingly or unknowingly, precipitate the pressure. After all, pressure brings the pleasure associated with their uptime. The key to determining whether you have the Pressure trait or are simply a procrastinator is recognizing whether you do your best work under pressure.

A Manager's Guide to Productivity Traits

Understanding Pressure traits can help your organization function more effectively. Suppose, for example, you have two salespeople working for you, one with the Pressure trait and one with the Non-Pressure trait. Now suppose you give them both yearly quotas. The salesperson with the Non-Pressure trait will sell a little at a time all year long—the chart showing his revenues will have no peaks and no valleys. But the salesperson with the Pressure trait will be a different story. Most of his sales will come in at the end of the year; and your manufacturing department will go crazy because it will be overwhelmed with orders.

The good news is that there's an easy solution. Once you recognize individuals' traits, you can manage salespeople with the Pressure trait by giving them monthly or quarterly quotas. They will sell during the last week of the month or the last month of the quarter, offering some consistency in the pace of orders for manufacturing. And what about the salespeople with the Non-Pressure trait? They need yearly quotas that allow them to set a consistent pace, without the pressure.

Managing these traits can help each person to function more effectively, but a person with the Pressure trait can still be either a strong salesperson or a lousy one. So can the person with the Non-Pressure trait. The Pressure and Non-Pressure traits don't tell how *well* a person will do, just how he will approach the job.

Can You Dance Together When You Have Different Rhythms?

If you have the Pressure trait, you may leave your part of a project to the next-to-the-last minute, then turn it over to a secretary with the Non-Pressure trait to complete by the end of the day. This won't strike you as a hardship; you're providing her with a terrific opportunity to be a recognized part of the team and feel that wonderful rush of adrenaline!

Sure you are. The trouble is, she won't see it that way. And you'll be setting her up for failure.

Never tell someone with the Non-Pressure trait, "We're in a crisis! Skip lunch!" If you do, that person will not function effectively. He might even say, "I have to get something to eat. I feel shaky." He's not trying to give you a hard time or be uncooperative; his body just doesn't react well to missing breaks.

If an individual with the Pressure trait is working with someone with the Non-Pressure trait in a crisis, the one with the Pressure trait may skip breakfast and lunch and work straight through. Someone with the Pressure trait often eats only one or two meals a day. If he's not aware of his coworker's Non-Pressure needs, the worker with the Pressure trait may say, "Don't you care about this project? You're going to lunch? You must not be committed. Are you lazy?"

Instead, the employee with the Pressure trait should say to the coworker with the Non-Pressure trait, "Why don't you take a break and get something to eat? I'll meet you back here in 20 minutes."

*While Judy worked all night, Carl took breaks for drinks
and snacks and finally, around 11:30 at night, said,
"I'm going to bed."*

That way both can maintain optimal work levels.

When Carl and his wife, Judy, were wallpapering their living room,
hall, and dining room, they followed this approach. Carl, who had
the Non-Pressure trait, took breaks for drinks and snacks and finally,
around 11:30 at night, said, "I'm going to bed." Judy, who had the
Pressure trait, continued working all night. She liked doing things
in one fell swoop, and she was still wallpapering when Carl rejoined
her at 7:30 the next morning. She understood Carl's work habits, and
it didn't bother her that they were different from hers.

Look at the Product, Not the Process

People with the Pressure trait sometimes have to contend with
Non-Pressure individuals who, believing that "normal is what I
am," consider the approach of the person with the Pressure trait to
be just plain wrong.

Typically, the Non-Pressure worker looks at the Pressure worker
in uptime and says, "You're a procrastinator. You don't care. You're

willing to settle for something that's average when it could be great."
Because the person with the Non-Pressure trait couldn't do a good
job at the last minute, he assumes that the one with the Pressure trait
can't either. He wants the employee with the Pressure trait to start
everything ahead of time, as he would himself. But if Pressure individuals start ahead of time, they work only to average—not optimal—levels. If forced, someone with the Pressure trait will start
ahead of time and even finish the project early. But then she'll typically redo the project in a last-minute crunch, because the last
minute is when she's most creative.

So what's the person with the Non-Pressure trait to do when
teamed with someone who has the Pressure trait? Back off. As long
as the work gets done on time and done well—and as long as the
other person doesn't insist that you adopt his approach—try not
to criticize his way of getting it done. Judy didn't blame Carl for going to bed, and Carl didn't get angry with Judy for going ahead
without him or not coming to bed.

The Pressure Trait and Organizations

Organizations need to recognize that if a Pressure employee has
been working in uptime on a project for a long time, that employee
needs some downtime before starting the next project. Some organizations are notorious for a "burn-'em-up, spit-'em-out" approach. Because those organizations don't allow for downtime,
employees leave in a very different condition from when they came
in. Apart from the human toll, these organizations are increasing
their personnel costs with that kind of turnover. It takes time and
money to search for and train new employees.

Matching the Pressure Trait to the Job

If you're someone with the Non-Pressure trait, you wouldn't do
well in a job fighting forest fires. In a job like that, it wouldn't be
unusual for you to be called on to fight a fire for eight hours straight,

and you wouldn't be able to go for coffee when you needed it. If you want to be involved with fighting forest fires and are a Non-Pressure individual, then you should look for an administrative job.

The Pressure and Non-Pressure traits are important considerations in all kinds of work environments. When Ian, a doctor, came in for a consultation with Judi, he looked as though he had the weight of the world on his shoulders. Ian had the Non-Pressure trait and was working in the emergency room of a busy hospital. Judi said, "So when they wheel in the five accident victims all at once, you go out for a cup of coffee." He sat up and said, "How did you know? I have to get something to eat before I can deal with it. The nurses think I'm awful."

Ian was a wonderful doctor—clear-headed and a great communicator—but he was not the right doctor for an emergency room or operating room. He needed a practice in which he could pace his patients and take short breaks. Being a doctor was not the problem; the problem was being a doctor in an emergency room. Ian's Non-Pressure trait wasn't bad, but it wasn't appropriate for the situation he was in.

To achieve success, you must know your trait and place yourself in the right situation for that trait. It is the responsibility of both

What's the Difference?

	Pressure	Non-Pressure
Gets the work done with:	pressure	pacing
Performs best:	in uptime	in normal time
Needs:	downtime	breaks, lead time
Views opposite type as:	uncaring, uncommitted	procrastinator, poor planner
Can manage self by:	applying own pressure	taking breaks; planning ahead
Managed by:	setting series of deadlines	allowing plenty of lead time

Get It in Writing

The amount of pressure you exert in your handwriting reveals your Pressure trait. Sounds easy, right? Well, it does take some time to get good at recognizing the middle of the range, but the extremes are easy to spot—and it's the extremes that are most important.

You can literally feel the pressure generated by a writer who has a strong Pressure trait. That person usually will push down so hard that you can easily make out the line of his writing on the other side of the paper. That 3-D effect doesn't come through on the printed page, of course, but the heavy pressure still shows in this sample.

*wee original sample 1st line
in case we can come we
executive search Desine*

Someone with a strong Non-Pressure trait will write so lightly that it's not always easy for readers to make out the characters. This is what that writing looks like. It is light and wispy.

*won't snorkeling for the
as old as of February
How about lunch Thursday?*

Most of us fall somewhere in the continuum between the extreme Pressure trait and the extreme Non-Pressure trait. The following sample illustrates average handwriting for someone who can work three to five hours straight before taking a break.

*is in now but I am
samples of handwriting done
handed. I hope you're able to*

the employer and the employee to understand their respective approaches to work and to assign job responsibilities accordingly.

In Short

We all need our breaks to do our best work, but those with the Pressure trait need them only after many hours, while those with the Non-Pressure trait need them at regular and frequent intervals. Many people can work perfectly well under pressure, but only true Pressure people actually thrive on it and really need it to do their best work.

Problems occur when we don't recognize opposite traits for what they are—traits. Not shiftless, lazy behavior; not lack of commitment; not lack of consideration; not procrastination. When you judge someone's behavior, we ask that you look at the result, not the process. Of course, if the process means that a project involving a ton of work and a tight deadline gets dumped on you, a Non-Pressure employee, then you need to show this chapter to the Pressure boss who is doing the dumping.

Chapter Three

Autonomy

Unfinished business

S HERRY, A COMPANY PRESIDENT, was told by her vice president that the executive team had developed a new marketing strategy while she was away on a business trip. Sherry sat through the presentation of the new plan, tapping her fingernails on the table the whole time. When the presentation was completed, she summarily rejected the whole thing—even though, she ruefully acknowledged to Judi later, "It was a darned good plan!"

Autonomy
Who Are You?
After each question, circle the answer
that comes closest to describing you.

1. Instead of being in the spotlight, I prefer being "behind the scenes."
a) Always
b) Sometimes
c) Never

2. I like to feel important or noticed.
a) Always
b) Sometimes
c) Never

3. "Most people do not know enough about what they are talking about, so I don't really need to listen to them." This describes my feelings.
a) Always
b) Sometimes
c) Rarely

4. I've been told I'm not a good listener.
a) Frequently
b) Occasionally
c) Rarely

5. I tend to think I'm right and seldom admit I'm wrong—or so people have told me.
a) Often
b) Occasionally
c) Rarely

6. If something goes wrong, it's the other person's fault.

a) Usually
b) Sometimes
c) Rarely

7. When I'm lost, I ask for directions.
a) Always
b) Sometimes
c) Rarely

8. Before anyone makes a decision in my family or work environment, I want to be consulted.
a) Always
b) Sometimes
c) Only if the decision relates to me

9. I'm comfortable with others coming into my house or work situation and giving me advice.
a) Usually
b) Sometimes
c) Rarely

10. If my spouse or significant other said, "Let's go to Restaurant X for dinner," I would feel like
a) going to Restaurant Y instead, even though I like them both equally.
b) going to either Restaurant X or Restaurant Y.
c) immediately accepting the other person's suggestion.

Sherry sat through the presentation of the new plan, tapping her fingernails on the table the whole time.

Sherry had just realized that she had a high Autonomy trait. People at the high end of the Autonomy trait continuum exhibit a number of characteristic behaviors that allow others to identify them easily. What sometimes is difficult is recognizing this trait in *yourself.*

The Autonomy trait may grow or shrink all through our lives,

SCORING
Add up your total score, using the following values for your answers.

1.	a) 0	b) 2	c) 5	5.	a) 5	b) 4	c) 0
2.	a) 5	b) 2	c) 0	6.	a) 5	b) 2	c) 0
3.	a) 5	b) 2	c) 0	7.	a) 0	b) 2	c) 5
4.	a) 5	b) 2	c) 0	8.	a) 5	b) 2	c) 0
				9.	a) 0	b) 2	c) 5
				10.	a) 5	b) 3	c) 0

If you score between 0 and 15, you are at the low end of the Autonomy trait continuum. A score between 16 and 30 means you are in the middle range. If you score higher than 30, you have a high Autonomy trait—and your coworkers would like you to read this chapter!

depending upon circumstances. Parents will not be surprised to learn that high Autonomy is first noticeable around age two and that it has another peak in the preteen and teenage years. The toddler and adolescent years are times when a child starts to realize her potential as an independent individual and wants to exert control over what she perceives as her domain.

"Mine! Mine! All Mine!"

The person with a high Autonomy trait has an attitude of ownership whether or not that attitude is matched by reality. It's the attitude a child, especially a teenager, has toward her room. The parents actually own the room, but from the child's point of view it is her room; she refers to "my bed" or "my dresser." A teenager feels she has the right to do whatever she wants to do in her room—decorate it, play loud music, or make a mess. Heaven forbid that a parent should contradict that assumption!

Still, the reality is that the room does not belong to the child; it belongs to the parents. When the child graduates from college (or finally leaves home ten years later), the parents will turn the room into a den or hobby room. If the parents sell the house, the child won't get money for her room. It never really *was* her room—but that minor detail won't keep her from expressing an attitude of ownership toward it.

Now let's take this same attitude into the work environment. If you divide an organization into departments or divisions and you assign an area to a person having at least a moderate Autonomy trait, that individual will display the attitude of ownership. She will begin to refer to the area in terms of "my" area, "my" people, "my" customers, "my" projects, "my" office, and "my" desk. She really does not own any of it—but she feels as if she does.

"Hey! Look at Me!"

The higher the Autonomy trait, the more an individual needs attention and needs to feel important. Someone with a very high Autonomy trait tends to feel comfortable in the spotlight, giving presentations. That's why we often find a high Autonomy trait in trial lawyers, actors, politicians, trainers, and other people who actually enjoy public speaking.

Things need to revolve around the very high Autonomy person, *whether it is in a positive or a negative way*, because then the high Autonomy person feels important. One of Hedy's clients employed an executive, Kerstin, who always managed to find a number of

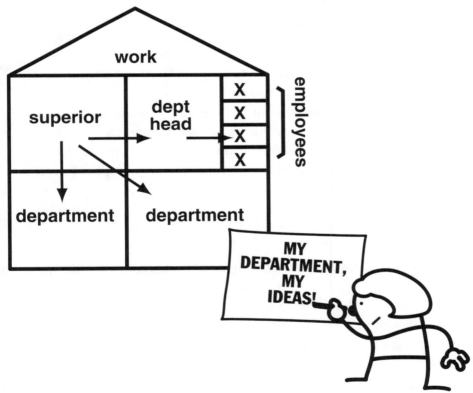

If you assign an area to a person having at least a moderate Autonomy trait, that individual will display the attitude of ownership.

critical responses to any situation or suggestion. Kerstin criticized subordinates (who were ready to quit) because they were "her" subordinates and she felt ownership of them. Her comments didn't stop there; she also criticized shortcomings in other departments. Despite the fact that Kerstin knew her remarks were not appreciated, she insisted on criticizing whether something was her business or not. What did she get? Attention. It didn't matter to her if it was negative; by causing controversy and anger, she made herself the center of attention.

Kerstin had valuable skills, and her boss didn't want to fire her if it could be avoided. The solution was to make her aware of her high Autonomy trait and help her learn to control the behaviors that resulted from it. The company also denied her attention when her comments were inappropriately negative and helped Kerstin to seek attention by more positive means.

As we've mentioned, not all cravings for attention are acted out in negative ways. Some people with high Autonomy get their attention on the stage or podium. Some need to be high achievers or extra nice. The point is that they need attention and will find a way to get it. The approach each person takes depends on the rest of his traits and values.

"It's Not Final Until I Say It's Final"

Another characteristic of the high Autonomy person is the need to feel important, to have the sense that she influences or controls her domain. Like the need for attention, this too can be acted out in different ways. Typically, though, the high Autonomy person feels she must have a say in everything concerning her perceived domain—from job candidates to corporate policies to product decisions to which college her child attends.

In the many years that Judi worked with outplaced executives, she heard frequent laments about the number of interviews required for certain positions. One company interviewed a candidate

20 times. Each interview was with a different executive, and each interview was lengthy. Why? A company that interviews this way has, in essence, stumbled onto the Autonomy trait. People in high places there know—though they might not express it this way—that high Autonomy individuals in the company need a say in everything. The person with high Autonomy feels compelled to put his stamp on each decision—and if he doesn't get the chance for that input, he will not accept the result (in this case the candidate who's hired). Those who understand traits know that they can manage this one by including everyone in the decision-making

One company interviewed a candidate 20 times, each time with a different executive. Why? High Autonomy people must give their input or they won't accept the result.

process. If each person has a say, the wise manager realizes, then each person also will have some ownership and will be more apt to go along with the decision.

Cartoonists who specialize in office humor have a field day with this trait. So do writers of situation comedies for television. After all, it's so obvious to everyone in the office! Even those who have the trait themselves recognize it in *others*. It just doesn't occur to them that *they* might have the same trait themselves.

The Autonomy Continuum

In the work environment, the attitude of ownership is easily recognized. Most people in any kind of managerial position have at least a moderate Autonomy trait; in essence, it's a requirement for the job. Without it, the individual will not have a "take-charge" attitude. Such a person will feel uncomfortable directing others. He will dislike being in the forefront and being the subject of all the attention associated with such a position. And what kind of a manager is that?

Like all traits, Autonomy operates on a continuum. To make it easier to recognize this one and talk about it, we will discuss the trait in terms of low, medium, and high Autonomy. In everyday life, the high and low ends are the easiest to recognize. We will consider the advantages and disadvantages of each, focusing on their effects on organizations, colleagues, and other relationships.

Low Autonomy: The Power Behind the Throne

Low Autonomy is typified by an individual who feels that "I don't own it, so I'm not responsible. I need permission to do anything." That is not a take-charge attitude, and it is unusual to see such a person in a take-charge position. A person with low Autonomy may be highly competent—even brilliant—and outstandingly productive. She may know exactly what needs to be done, but she feels she needs permission to act. She lacks the "take-charge attitude" that comes with a sense of ownership, and she does not like the limelight. Only after a person with low Autonomy leaves the company do others realize how much she accomplished. In children with low Autonomy we have the opposite of the "squeaky-wheel syndrome"; these are the kids who do not get noticed.

Then there's the positive side. Low Autonomy people generally don't ruffle feathers (assuming they have other complementary traits), because they consult others before doing anything. They are willing to accept good ideas that do not originate with them. They may even be good team players because they don't have to be in control. It was a wise person who observed, "You can accomplish anything if you do not need to take credit for it." And if we knew who that person was, we'd give her credit.

Because the low Autonomy person shuns the limelight, he's likely to be found working behind the scenes. This person may be the real power behind the high Autonomy boss, or he may be just a reliable worker. However, avoiding the limelight does not necessarily mean the low Autonomy worker wants to avoid promotions and raises. Frequently such an employee does not want to draw attention to himself by creating a fuss. He feels uncomfortable putting himself in a position in which he receives attention for his accomplishments—and then feels unappreciated as he is passed over again and again in favor of less capable but more self-promoting colleagues. That employee is likely to be silently frustrated at work, but may not be so silent in his work-related complaints to friends and family.

The low Autonomy person needs to learn to promote himself, even though this goes against his instincts. In a job interview this person automatically tends to downplay his accomplishments instead of emphasizing what he has done. Refusing to put on any airs, he is likely to present himself in a humble rather than an exaggerated way. The result? He can appear to the interviewer to be less competent than he really is.

If a low Autonomy person wants the job, he needs to grit his teeth and document his past successes. On the other side of the desk, interviewers can gain by recognizing that with low Autonomy applicants, what you see is what you get. You may even get more than what you immediately see, because the low Autonomy applicant is likely to downplay his accomplishments rather than exaggerate them. When you're the interviewer, you'll be most successful if you consider each applicant's statements about himself in the context of how high his Autonomy trait may be. And as you will see at the end of this chapter, it's not hard to identify that trait.

Once he gets the position, the low Autonomy employee who happens to have a high Autonomy boss needs to continue documenting his own accomplishments. Then he can bring out this documentation at review time to support a request for a raise. If that low Autonomy employee is you, and you still feel you're being passed over for promotions too often, you may need to learn to make yourself more visible. Sometimes it may even be helpful to practice public speaking or dressing for success.

Moderate Autonomy: The Happy Medium

An individual needs to have at least a moderate Autonomy trait—meaning that she has some sense of ownership—if she's to be given managerial responsibility. The typical manager, who has an Autonomy trait somewhere between moderate and high, begins to show ownership when she's assigned to her own area. This shows in her speech; she uses terms such as "my area," "my department," "my customers," etc. This sense of ownership is essential in a manager. If you have ever had a low Autonomy boss, you know how frustrating it can be to have a department for which no one takes responsibility. It's at that point that the inmates take over the asylum.

The person with moderate Autonomy usually takes charge, although there may be times when she does not. And she may not take the credit all the time either. So the degree to which a person with moderate Autonomy is noticed will depend upon other factors—how verbal, how outgoing, even how physically attractive she is.

A person can be at one extreme or the other of the Autonomy continuum, or anywhere in between. Someone who scores at the low end of moderate on the Autonomy scale will act more like the low Autonomy person; someone at the high end of moderate will act more like the high Autonomy person.

If there is ever a "happy medium" when it comes to traits, this is it—at least for the subordinates of these people. Someone with moderate Autonomy can assume enough responsibility and control to handle an executive position, but will rarely incur the kind of fury in her coworkers that the truly high Autonomy person often does.

High Autonomy: Turf, Tape, and Stamps

It is important to understand what is behind the high Autonomy trait, since the trait may be interpreted negatively by others. The high Autonomy person is not purposefully trying to harm others. Rather, he is reacting instinctively, based on his high Autonomy trait.

A high Autonomy trait is easy to spot, and anything in the *very* high range is unmistakable. That's the point at which the attitude of ownership that defines Autonomy reaches an extreme in "turf" issues. The need for attention—the other hallmark of high Autonomy—can lead the individual to demand and display status symbols and to require that he be consulted on all sorts of decisions. He may even hold up or interfere with decisions others have made. And that, of course, leads to all kinds of red tape in organizations.

When a person with very high Autonomy does not feel properly recognized in a work environment, she will prevent things from moving ahead. This was what happened when Sherry refused to accept the marketing program her executive team developed. Multiply this trait 20 times and you have the situation in which the job candidate was required to submit to 20 interviews. Can you imagine one candidate who would be entirely acceptable to that many people? But someone in that company knew that if any one of those 20 interviewers did *not* put his stamp of approval on the candidate, he would never accept that candidate. This is the kind of red tape that gives high Autonomy a bad name.

The high Autonomy person insists on being consulted and on

having his stamp on everything, but that does not necessarily mean he actually knows what to do. And it certainly doesn't automatically mean he's *good* at what he does. Those two things involve other traits. The high Autonomy manager could be, for example, indecisive and a poor implementer. His success might come largely as a result of working in conjunction with someone else—someone who is low on Autonomy but very competent. That person who is the power behind the high Autonomy throne doesn't want a lot of attention. Not so with the high Autonomy person!

Consider the case of the general and his assistant. The general wears the fancy uniform and goes to all the important meetings and social functions. It is the general's assistant who does the research, prepares the reports and paperwork, keeps the schedule organized, and always makes sure the general is in the right place at the right

The general could not be nearly as successful as he is without this behind-the-scenes help, but no one even knows the assistant's name.

time with the right information. The general could not be nearly as successful as he is without this behind-the-scenes help, but no one even knows the assistant's name.

All of the Credit, None of the Blame

The higher a person scores on the Autonomy scale, the more that person thinks he is *always right*. People with very high Autonomy are never wrong. If anything goes wrong, it is not the fault of the person with high Autonomy. It's someone else's fault. It's the economy's fault. It's *your* fault. . .

This is very comfortable for the high Autonomy person, but not always so great for others who interact with that person. When anything goes wrong in a relationship, the individual with the very high Autonomy trait always feels that it's the *other* person— spouse, subordinate, partner, or even superior—who is causing the problem. "*I* don't need to change," that person feels. "*We* don't need counseling; *you* need counseling." It's rare for the person with the very high Autonomy trait to take responsibility for problems. There is a time when he'll stop pointing fingers, however—he'll step right up as soon as it's time to take the credit for something going *right*.

When we told one client that he had a high Autonomy trait, he protested that that could not be right. He told us that when he and his wife were having problems, she was the one who refused counseling, so he went by himself. When we asked why he did that, he told us that he went to find out what was wrong with *her*. He took all the credit for trying.

Communicating Up the Ladder

A person with very high Autonomy usually relates to her superiors in one of two ways. Since she needs to feel important, she will either try to remain independent and separate, or she will align herself with someone in a position of power. Someone who takes the first approach may prefer working as far away from supervision as possible, so she can call the shots. She's likely to give out as little information as she can so no one will interfere with "her" area. Besides, she feels that she owns the area anyway, so it doesn't occur to her to tell her supervisor what is going on. This is often perceived as a lack of strong communication with superiors—but it is not necessarily an intentional holding back. The high Autonomy person feels that she's very capable of handling things and can be trusted. So it never crosses her mind to talk about what is happening.

Since this high Autonomy subordinate doesn't communicate a lot with the manager, the manager may go out of his way to find out what's happening. He may go into her area and start asking questions—at which point the subordinate physically tightens up. It's clear she doesn't want her manager checking up on her. That's a high Autonomy trait. It's natural for the subordinate literally to tighten up because she feels her superior's interest is an intrusion and sees it as demonstrating a lack of trust.

It doesn't make any difference if the supervisor has a high Autonomy trait, too. In that case, instead of understanding how his subordinate may feel, the supervisor will feel he has every right to go into his subordinate's area. After all, as manager, he feels he not only owns the department, but also is responsible for its success. The amount of freedom high Autonomy managers expect from their superiors is not what they give their subordinates. They tend to delegate the task but not the responsibility, ownership, or authority.

But let's get back to the high Autonomy subordinate. Sometimes, instead of fighting for separate turf, a high Autonomy employee will take the opposite approach. He may identify a power figure within an organization, align himself with that person, and derive his own power and prestige through that relationship. This high Autonomy individual likes becoming the confidante, adviser, or friend of the power figure and gains influence that way. He gains the attention he needs when others recognize this relationship and

A high Autonomy subordinate sometimes may align himself with a power figure and derive his own power and prestige through that relationship.

the power he craves when others need to go through him to get to the powerful person.

"My" Employees

If a manager has high Autonomy, he feels ownership of everything in his area of the organization—and that includes his subordinates. A high Autonomy manager will tell others in the company, "If you have anything to say to my people, say it to me and I'll talk to them." He needs to feel important and in control, so he insists that everything go through him.

Here's how that plays out. Say a subordinate prepares a report that has to go to an upper level. It is highly unlikely that the high Autonomy manager will let the subordinate present the report; instead, the manager will present it. If it is accepted, the high Autonomy manager will instinctively take the accolades and forget to mention that the subordinate did the work. Does the general say,

"The credit for this great work belongs to my assistant"? Yet if the report is rejected, the high Autonomy manager is quick to blame the subordinate. The general might say, "My assistant did not follow though properly. I will speak to him." This air of total confidence on the part of the high Autonomy person ensures that others feel confident in him.

On the other hand, it can lead to some agonizing situations. Andrew, for example, was a boss who had a terrible dilemma. Very high on Autonomy, he had presented the work of a subordinate, George, at a meeting. When the work was enthusiastically received, Andrew instinctively took credit. Later, however, George was in trouble with Andrew's superiors, who needed to downsize and thought George was expendable. Andrew liked and valued George, who was his right-hand person. He didn't want to lose him. Moreover, he wanted to use the work that had been so well received as an example of George's worth—but he didn't know how to get around having taken credit for himself. In the end, though Andrew felt terrible about it, George's job was eliminated. And all Andrew could do at that point was to give his former subordinate excellent references.

Rejection in Three Variations

Anyone with high Autonomy needs to see herself as having choice and control. The higher the Autonomy trait, the more likely the individual is to say no to any idea she didn't invent personally. The high Autonomy person has difficulty accepting finished ideas.

And what, exactly, is a finished idea? It's one in which the person on the receiving end has not had a choice or a chance for input. The idea has been completed without her participation. In general, people high on the Autonomy trait will respond to finished ideas in one of three ways.

1. The Flat-Out "No"

If you say to a person with high Autonomy, "Let's have pizza tonight," the high Autonomy person will feel compelled to say no. If you present a high Autonomy client with a set of totally completed plans—for an ad campaign, a building project, a policy change—the high Autonomy person will usually reject them. If you ask why he rejected your finished idea, he will come up with a rationalization. But that was not the real basis for the negative response; it was just a knee-jerk reaction to someone else's finished idea.

That's why Sherry said no to a plan she knew was excellent. She couldn't help herself; it was an instinctive response. She had had no part in developing the plan. She had not been consulted in the formative stages. It was presented to her as a finished idea.

Sometimes people with high Autonomy lack the power to just say no. This is true of children, for example, as well as subordinates. Neither of these groups has final decision-making power—but they do have two other options.

2. The Holdup

If you tell a high Autonomy subordinate to be at a meeting at 9:00 A.M., the subordinate might say, "Let me check my schedule and get back to you," even if she knows the time is free. The high Autonomy person cannot say yes right away. This is the overt variation of the holdup.

There is also the passive-aggressive variation. If you ask a high Autonomy subordinate to do a piece of work right away, the subordinate might say, "Fine," but put it on the back burner. He might delay it or submit it late. This is also the person who is chronically late to meetings that he did not plan.

3. The Switch

If a high Autonomy subordinate cannot use the holdup, she might try the switch. Tell a high Autonomy subordinate to be at a meeting at 9:00 A.M., and the subordinate will ask if it can't be 9:15. Suggest white paint for the walls in the new conference room, and the high Autonomy subordinate will want ivory. The high Autonomy person loves red pencils. She has to check everything. She may change only one word in a report, but she has to make her mark. The one word she changes may even mean exactly the same thing as the one she's replacing—but it's *her* word.

High Autonomy people hold up, change, or say no to any finished idea, no matter how excellent it is. This is not malicious. Really. It's instinctive, automatic behavior based on a trait.

But Wait! There's an Up Side!

It's easy to see why a high Autonomy manager can be resented by subordinates. But this trait can be useful—even essential—in certain situations. High Autonomy people always think they are right, for example, so if they are in sales, whatever they are selling has to be the best. They truly believe in the product or service, and they sell it with gusto. How could we not buy from them?

Politicians usually have high Autonomy. That's why they can say one thing one year, with absolute enthusiasm and commitment, and then say the opposite the next year with every bit as much conviction. Because they seem so certain of themselves, they're able to convince many people to follow them. It's called campaigning.

High Autonomy lawyers are absolutely convinced they can win even weak cases because they, having high Autonomy, are sure they are right and can't imagine being wrong. They have such belief in themselves that they are very convincing.

A doctor with high Autonomy can be comforting because she sounds so confident. This has a corresponding down side, however: She is not likely to listen to you if you ask for a particular test or treatment. In fact, that particular test or treatment will usually be the last one you'll get. (Remember the "holdup"?)

In employment interviews, applicants with the high Autonomy trait sound as though they have the world by the tail. They can do anything, and they have already accomplished wonders. They are convinced of these things, so they convince the interviewer. They are excellent salespeople for themselves. Perhaps you have met people like this. Perhaps you *are* one.

How to Deal with High Autonomy People

In a business setting, it is wise to assume that any manager has a very high Autonomy trait. It's safer, because that way you remember to present ideas in a way the manager will be able to accept.

So once you make that assumption, how do you act on it? Here are some strategies.

Present Only Unfinished Ideas

"Well, of course, this is just a draft. See what you think needs to be done."

If you err on the side of caution by assuming that everyone has a high Autonomy trait, you can present your proposals in such a way that people will be likely to respond positively. Judi once worked with Jeremiah, who was employed by an advertising firm and who had spent hours preparing a billboard idea for a client. The idea was excellent, but there was a problem—the client had a very high Autonomy trait. Judi told Jeremiah that he wasn't going to get approval because the idea was too finished. There was nothing for the client to change; he could only hold it up. But Jeremiah didn't want to spend any more time on the project. Judi told him, "OK, you have to present it as unfinished."

He responded, "But it's *not* unfinished; it's finished!"

Judi explained, "*We* know it's finished, but you have to present it as unfinished. What you need to do is make your presentation but say, 'This is a rough draft; this is not a finished project. I want you to look at it and tell me what you want me to do differently.' Of course, the client doesn't know about art or advertising. He won't know what to do, but you need to give him the option."

So Jeremiah told his client that the design was a rough draft. The client walked around the table, looked at it, walked around the table some more, and looked at it some more. He didn't know what to change or switch because there really *was* nothing to be changed or switched. He left the room and walked around outside for awhile, then returned to the room and said, "It's fine." He was actually annoyed that there was no way to change the design. But he was able to hold it up for a while, which made him feel he had control.

Whenever we see a married couple in which one person has a very high Autonomy trait, the other has usually learned to present ideas in unfinished terms. "What do you think about having a dinner party?" that spouse will say. "Do you think 20 or so?" Once you have given high Autonomy people a choice like this, they may be willing to let you work out the details.

Give Her a Chance to Put Her Stamp on It

One of Judi's clients, Howard, was one of several urban designers competing for a big project. Each designer was given money to prepare a design, then the one whose design was selected would win the lucrative contract. The official who was to select the design rejected them all. Six months and several submissions later, Howard was in despair. He couldn't afford to spend more time redesigning,

Howard gave the official the chance to make a minor change, to put her stamp on it, and within two days his design was accepted.

only to be rejected. Judi suggested that he present the design to the official in its existing form and ask, "What do I need to change in this design to get this contract signed?" This implied an unfinished design and gave the official the chance to make a switch, to put her stamp on it. She made a minor change, and within two days Howard's design was accepted; he was awarded the contract.

Present a Red Herring

Judi's client Ed was a landscape designer for town commons and municipal areas. With work like this, it is typically a committee that hires the designer and a committee that decides if the completed work is acceptable. The usual process was that Ed would present his entire design, get it approved, and complete the project. Then the committee would have to come and inspect his work before he got paid.

Of course, most committees have their share of high Autonomy people, and those people have to say no, hold up, or change something. So they would delay paying him, because in their minds, there was always something wrong. The notion of *what* was wrong was different according to each high Autonomy member, you understand, but they all agreed that *something* needed to be changed. Time after time it would take an eternity for Ed to get paid.

When Ed told Judi about the situation, Judi suggested introducing a red herring. The red herring approach means presenting the project with a major flaw—on purpose. The flaw gives all the high Autonomy members the same clear object to focus on, and since you have chosen it yourself, you can be prepared to fix it quickly. It also commits the group to granting approval once that flaw has been corrected.

Here's how it worked for Ed: when it was time for the committee to inspect, he would have a tree planted in the middle of a sidewalk, or include some other feature that was equally outrageous. Everything else would be absolutely beautiful, but there would be this tree in the middle of the sidewalk. All the committee members

***When dealing with a high Autonomy person, put something
outrageous in the job for her to focus on and change.***

would seize upon the placement of the tree. "Of course, we can't
approve the project this way!" they'd say.

Ed would then ask them, "Does anything else have to be changed,
or is that what is holding up approval?"

"Yes, that's what's holding it up," all would reply.

Ed would have his crew ready with a bulldozer and cement to fix
the problem before their eyes. The committee had already said that
the placement of the tree was what was holding up approval, and
that when it was fixed, he could get his check. It was, and he did.

This approach works in other lines of work, too. Some lawyers
include red herrings when they write contracts so that people with
high Autonomy will have something insignificant to change and
will stay away from the big stuff.

Of course, the red herring is a ploy you can use only when you
don't deal with the same people all the time. But if it's a one-time
deal, like a contract, put something outrageous in there for the
high Autonomy client to focus on and change.

Document Everything

It can be interesting to be the subordinate of a very high Autonomy boss. It certainly doesn't take long to learn that everything must go through the boss. After all, he feels that he owns not only the department but also *you* as a part of that department. This approach comes from more than just the attitude of ownership; it also reflects the real need of the high Autonomy boss to get attention and place his stamp on everything.

As we've discussed, the high Autonomy boss is quick to accept credit for a subordinate's work and is equally quick to transfer blame. As infuriating as it is, this is instinctive, automatic behavior, not calculated to hurt the subordinate. Still, the result is the same: when a scapegoat is needed, you'll probably be it. Be prepared.

How do you do that? Document everything. Keep records of what you do, take notes on conversations, hold on to instructions the boss gives you. In addition to supporting a request for a raise or promotion, such documentation will also put you in a better position to defend yourself to the boss—or the boss's boss—if necessary.

"Who, Me?" or What to Do If You Have a High Autonomy Trait

When we talk with people who have high Autonomy traits, they usually don't think that they have them. They typically deny "doing that." But if we press further and ask how they react in certain circumstances, then they will agree. Of course, if a spouse or coworker is with the high Autonomy individual, that person will often say, "That's *exactly* what you do!"

It is unlikely that you can be objective about whether you have this trait. If you see it in your handwriting, you need to ask people you trust to tell you honestly if you frequently reject ideas when you have not participated in forming them, present subordinates' plans as your own, or blame others for things that go wrong. Are you accused of not being a good listener, of thinking you are always right, of not communicating well with superiors, or of being a "know-it-all"? If you answer yes to any of these questions—or earned a high score on the quiz at the beginning of this chapter—then chances are you have a high Autonomy trait. So how can you manage it?

Recognize and Accept It

Since high Autonomy people typically resist ideas that come from someone else, you get major points just for recognizing and accepting that you have a high Autonomy trait. You know that, like any other trait, it has both helpful and unhelpful aspects. Once you have accepted that you have the trait, you can enjoy its advantages and mitigate its disadvantages.

Ask for Help

Yes, this is very hard. For some people, it's very, *very* hard. Asking for help runs against the grain of high Autonomy people. That is why they are so resistant to counseling. However, by now you realize that others recognize your high Autonomy trait, only that's not what they call it. They probably have some considerably less flattering names for it. They may even assume you are intentionally out to hurt them. If you acknowledge the trait and explain it to them, you will be much more likely to gain their respect and cooperation than if you deny it.

Tell people, "I have a high Autonomy trait, and this is the effect it has. When you come and tell me your idea, my instinctive, unthinking response is to say no. So when you come and tell me your ideas, if I say 'no' right away, will you tell me? Ask, 'Could this be your high Autonomy trait? Before you say no, let's just think about the idea for the idea's sake.' " (Of course, when you explain the trait to subordinates, you might want to mention all its negative *and* positive aspects.)

High Autonomy is not a trait you can take care of on your own because it causes you to respond automatically—and the stronger the trait, the more instantaneous the response. So if you can make sure that the people around you know you have it, they can help you become more aware of it and control it, and they will have greater respect for you.

We tell supervisors, "You may always think you're right. Every time a subordinate brings you an idea, you may reject it or hold it up. If you do, in time subordinates will stop bringing suggestions to you. They will think, 'What's the point?'" If you are part of upper management, you will limit the creativity of your team and maybe even your organization.

Laugh

You really have to have a sense of humor about a high Autonomy trait. Along with accepting it, make a conscious effort to laugh about it. That's not easy, because the instinctive response when someone tells you about the effect of your high Autonomy trait is to get annoyed. But it's important to substitute a new behavior when trying to break a habit. Besides, your subordinates will probably be more than happy to point out the humor in the situation!

Keep on Top of It

Controlling your traits is like dyeing your hair. You have to stay aware of it and on top of it, or the natural way keeps coming through. And the best way to stay attuned to your traits is to have people help you, because you will forget. (Don't we all?) This is especially important for people scoring high on the Autonomy trait, who are less likely than those with other traits to ask for help.

Another way to control this trait is actually to practice giving credit to subordinates who deserve it. You'll need to plan ahead for this, because if you don't, you will instinctively take credit.

Autonomy in the Organization

The Autonomy trait can be useful in situations in which you wish to sell a product or an idea to others. Remember that thinking you are right causes you to sell with gusto and confidence. Others follow your lead and buy in to your thinking. If you want to be in sales—or law or politics, which are really sales under other names—this is an extremely positive trait to have. As we've said, it can work well for doctors, too. When it becomes problematic is when people have to work together. So whether you're creating a department or just a temporary committee, it's always a good idea to have a mix of high, moderate, and low Autonomy members. After all, you know that if five high Autonomy people are on a committee and one makes a suggestion, the others will never be able simply to agree.

Since the high Autonomy people never admit making mistakes, when something goes wrong in an organization made up of high Autonomy people, everyone immediately points a finger at someone else. The Iran-Contra affair is an example of many pointed fingers. If you've ever worked in an organization in which something went wrong—and who hasn't?—did you notice how quickly people pointed fingers at everyone else?

This trait can cause red tape and stall innovation and implementation in the organization. After all, this is the trait that requires 20 different people to approve a new hire. It plays out in other expensive ways, too. We've all seen new executives bring their own people when they come into an organization. Sometimes a clean sweep is exactly what's needed. Other times the problem is not that the current employees are incompetent; it's that they are, in a sense, finished ideas. The high Autonomy executive has to make changes, to exercise choice and control.

As participants in such situations have learned to their chagrin, this trait costs organizations millions of dollars. To avoid such losses, executives need to be aware of their own Autonomy traits; recognize their automatic, instinctive behaviors; and change those behaviors when appropriate. They also need to be aware of the Autonomy traits of their employees in order to catch red tape, holdups, and possible blocks to creativity. Most important, the high Autonomy person must acknowledge and discuss the trait with coworkers. They'll have to appreciate your self-awareness if you ask, "Is this why we've been sitting here for two hours unable to make a de-

What's the Difference?

High Autonomy	Low Autonomy
Refers to "my" department, client, customer, project, etc., as opposed to "the" department, etc.	Needs permission
Displays an attitude of ownership	Does not take charge
Needs to be noticed	Tends to stay behind the scenes
Needs to feel he has choices and control	Doesn't need control
Has difficulty accepting finished ideas	Can easily accept finished ideas
Has a consistent and intense desire to put a "stamp" on every decision	Does not have to be involved in everything or have a "stamp" on decisions
Automatically responds to others' ideas with "No," the "Holdup," or the "Switch"	Accepts others' ideas on merit alone

What to Do If You Are High Autonomy	What to Do If You Are Low Autonomy
Identify and accept it.	If you want promotions or raises, learn to promote yourself or identify a high Autonomy person who will do it for you.
Ask for help.	
Laugh a lot.	Document your contributions.
Keep on top of it.	
Plan ahead to acknowledge subordinates' contributions.	
Remember the positive side of it.	

cision?" The first step to overcoming the negative effects of high Autonomy is to admit it is present.

Knowledge is power.

In Short

A low Autonomy trait can be a problem for those who have it because they may not get the raises or promotions they deserve. They may be perceived as less assertive and less credible than their peers

Get It in Writing

People with high Autonomy like to be noticed, to stand out in the crowd.
Their signatures stand out, too. You can't tell much about a person's
Autonomy trait if you see his signature in isolation. But you can tell a
lot if you compare the overall expanse of the signature to that
of the rest of the writing.

A person whose signature is much larger than the "crowd" of the text is
signifying a feeling of importance or a desire to be noticed. That's an individual with high Autonomy.

A signature smaller than the size of the writing in the text indicates that
this person would rather not be noticed but would prefer to stay in the
background. This suggests low Autonomy.

The signature of someone with moderate Autonomy, not surprisingly, is
the same size as or slightly larger than the text.

and as lacking self-confidence. However, they also are often perceived as natural and down-to-earth.

It's a *high* Autonomy trait that's problematic for everyone involved. For both those who have it and those who have to deal with it, high Autonomy is one of the most misunderstood, misinterpreted, and mishandled traits of all. People often refer to it in not-so-glowing terms when they describe someone as "egotistical," "self-serving," "a show-off," "cocky," "a know-it-all," "a kiss-up," or "dishonest." There are also very complimentary terms for the Autonomy trait; that's often what we're referring to when we call someone "confident," "self-assured," "convincing," "independent," or "gutsy." These terms describe behavior without the underlying trait or the underlying motivation.

Cartoonists depict this trait more than any other precisely because it is so often noticed, yet so rarely understood or appropriately handled. It's important to guard against the tendency to assume that someone with a high Autonomy trait is "out to get" his subordinates; his actions are merely the automatic and instinctive results of a trait. Once aware of the trait and the behaviors that result from it, we can determine whether the behaviors are beneficial or detrimental in a particular situation. This awareness will allow far greater choices for both those with the trait and those interacting with them.

If you're dealing with someone who is unaware of his high Autonomy trait, try these strategies:

1. Present your ideas as being unfinished.
2. Give the person the chance to put his stamp on the idea.
3. If you expect to be dealing with that particular person (or group) only once, include a red herring when you make your presentation.
4. If you think there could be a finger-pointing session later, document everything.

Finally, take the time to treat everyone you deal with as if you know he's at the high end of the Autonomy continuum. It takes more time in the beginning but saves so much time, money, and energy in the end.

Chapter Four

Internal Direction and External Direction

"I know what to do"

THE PRESIDENT OF A COMPANY we'll call Whatsits Inc. had recently hired a new vice president. Yet only a few months later, the president wanted to fire him. "This guy is always in my office asking me what to do!" he complained to Judi. "I say, 'Look, that's what I'm paying you for. You go make the decision; you should be able to do it!'" Despite the expense and difficulty entailed, he was ready to fire the vice president.

Internal Direction and External Direction
Who Are You?

After each question, circle the answer that comes closest to describing you.

1. When it comes to making decisions, I find myself vacillating.
a) Very seldom
b) Sometimes
c) Usually

2. I like my supervisor to tell me what needs to be done.
a) Usually
b) Occasionally when I am not sure
c) Almost never

3. Some people, after finishing a project, tend to wait for the boss to explain what should be done next. This describes me
a) always.
b) rarely; I figure out what to do next, and go ahead.
c) sometimes, and other times I proceed on my own.

4. Some people are leaders and some are followers. I'd describe myself as
a) a natural leader; people always look to me.
b) somewhere in the middle; I don't necessarily take charge, but I could if necessary.
c) a team member; I'm rarely the leader.

5. If asked to characterize my expectations of others at work, I'd say that
a) I try to act like an adult and carry my own workload. I think others should do the same and am frustrated when somebody wants his hand held.
b) I know not everyone is a decision maker, so I am prepared to help other employees and serve as a mentor.
c) I often need help with decisions myself, so I understand when others need the same kind of assistance.

6. Some people are frequently frustrated at work when they find themselves asked to do things that they feel will take the organization in the wrong direction. In terms of my own experience,
a) this happens often.
b) this happens sometimes.
c) this happens seldom, since I do not usually have a firm opinion on what should be done.

7. When it comes to direction,
a) it's easier for me to give it than take it.
b) I can both give it and take it easily.
c) I would rather take direction than give it.

Another president, this one in charge of a company we'll call Whosits, complained to Judi that when he gave direction to *his* second in command, the fellow argued with him about whether that was what should be done. This president, too, was upset and wanted to get rid of his VP.

If the two presidents could have traded vice presidents, both might have been happy. Why? What's behind the dissatisfaction, of course, is not something wrong with the vice presidents or something wrong with the presidents, but something about the mix of

8. Given a choice, I am apt to go along with what others want to do
a) usually, because I don't have another plan.
b) sometimes, but on other occasions I have another suggestion for them.
c) rarely; often I come up with a plan and want them to go along with me.

9. Sometimes I see a coworker complete a task and then wait to be told what the next task will be, instead of moving to it on his own. Typically my response to that situation is that
a) I wonder why he can't figure out what needs to be done next.
b) this sometimes happens to me, so I can understand it.
c) I totally understand this because it happens to me often.

10. Given a choice, I prefer making decisions with others, rather than on my own.
a) Usually
b) Sometimes
c) Rarely

SCORING
Add up your total score, using the following values for your answers.

1.	a) 5	b) 2	c) 0
2.	a) 0	b) 2	c) 5
3.	a) 0	b) 5	c) 2
4.	a) 5	b) 2	c) 0
5.	a) 3	b) 5	c) 0
6.	a) 5	b) 3	c) 0
7.	a) 5	b) 2	c) 0
8.	a) 0	b) 3	c) 5
9.	a) 5	b) 3	c) 0
10.	a) 0	b) 2	c) 5

A score of 0 through 20 means you're high on External Direction. Anything from 21 through 40 indicates moderate Internal Direction, and a score of 41 or higher indicates high Internal Direction.

"This guy is always in my office asking me what to do!"
The president was ready to fire his vice president.

Another president complained, "This guy is always arguing
with my orders!" He, too, was ready to fire his vice president.

their traits. Once they learned this, each team was able to work together effectively.

Without an understanding of traits, it sometimes seems there is
just no pleasing people. But a knowledge of the Internal Direction
and External Direction traits explains a lot of the conflicts and

problems encountered both at work and in relationships. These two traits shed a new light on some people who seem stubborn and others who appear lazy or uncaring.

The Internal Direction and External Direction traits give us vital information about how you work with a group and by yourself. They explain:

- Your natural place on a team: leader, peer, or follower.
- How strongly you hold to your idea of the right direction to go.
- How you make decisions. (Do you figure things out yourself? Do you ask others? Do you like to run ideas by others for feedback? Are you most comfortable working things out with a team?)

Decisions, Decisions

Picture a train coming down a railroad track. It comes to a point where it can go in any of several directions. Inside the locomotive is an engineer who decides how fast to go, when to stop, and which track to go on next. We would call the train Internally Directed because direction is coming from inside the train.

But there are also other trains that are run by computers or by switching houses someplace else. It is the computer that tells these trains how fast to go, when to stop, and which track to go on next. We would call this type of train Externally Directed because its directions are coming from outside the train.

A small company had only one secretary, Anna. She knew that she was responsible for typing, filing, answering the phone, and billing. When she was totally caught up on these activities, she sat at her desk looking at magazines. Or if the bosses were around, she asked if there was anything that needed to be done. Then Externally Directed Anna left the company, and Internally Directed Deb was hired for the same position. Once she'd learned the office system, Deb, like Anna, occasionally found herself with time on her hands

Inside the locomotive is an engineer who decides how fast to go, when to stop, and which track to go on next.

after she had completed her assigned tasks. So Deb decided to organize the storeroom. After that was done, she created an office manual on procedures and where to find supplies. She didn't need to ask what had to be done or how to do it; she could decide for herself. Sounds like the ideal employee, right? Well, maybe not. It all depends on the situation.

The Decision Continuum

Everyone's traits fall somewhere on a continuum from high Internal Direction to high External Direction. Complicating things still further, it's entirely possible for an individual to fall closer to the Internally Directed end of the continuum in some areas of his life and closer to the Externally Directed end in other areas. Many people are in the middle—neither strongly Internally Directed nor strongly Externally Directed. A person in the middle of the continuum prefers making important decisions jointly with peers. He will know what to do sometimes but not all the time. Such a person

But there are also other trains that are run by computers or by switching houses someplace else.

is called a "natural peer." As a manager, his philosophy will be that we all are equal; we're all adults; we each should carry our own share of the workload. He will become frustrated with an employee who wants to have his hand held. A natural peer does not want to teach for too long or mentor; he prefers working with people who know their jobs and "just get it done" without a lot of close management.

Let's look a little more closely at each end of the continuum. When a highly Internally Directed person finishes a task, she will consider what should be done next, make a decision, and act on it. Such a person is often seen as a "natural leader."

There are two kinds of natural leaders. The first kind is used to having people follow her. She accepts the fact that others sometimes need to have their hands held a bit. In fact, she tends to enjoy

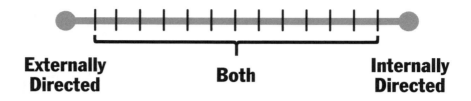

Everyone's traits fall somewhere on a continuum from high Internal Direction to high External Direction.

mentoring or taking someone "under her wing." The other kind of natural leader also knows what to do next, but she expects that others will instinctively know how to proceed too—and she becomes impatient when they don't. She likes to be surrounded by people who are cooperative, who do not give her a hard time about which direction to go. Of course, she may forget to *tell* them what to do, assuming that they already know. She expects people to be like her and know what to do next with little or no direction.

Then there's the other extreme: an Externally Directed person who completes a task, but is not sure what to do next and doesn't want to do the wrong thing. The Externally Directed person needs to ask someone else's opinion; if and only if he receives a reasonable answer, he proceeds. But until then, the Externally Directed person stays in neutral, not moving ahead because he is unsure what to do next. If there is no place to go for direction, he just marks time. The person with the External Direction trait is seen as a "natural follower" and will assume that role in most situations. He can be perceived as having low motivation, since he doesn't seem to have the initiative to move ahead on his own. In fact, however, what's causing this behavior is not low motivation but merely a lack of direction.

Internal Direction: The Good News

All traits have advantages and disadvantages, depending on the requirements of the situation, but this shows up especially clearly with the Internal Direction trait. The positive side of being Internally Directed is that the employee with this trait doesn't need much supervision. She knows what to do next and can make decisions. As soon as one assignment is complete, she goes on to the next.

An employee who is Internally Directed will have a tendency to attract people who need direction; others sense that she can make decisions and they come to her for advice. If she gives good advice, then people will tend to follow her and she'll be seen as a leader. Internally Directed people are often the de facto leaders of their groups even when they don't have that official designation.

A word of caution here: while individuals high on this trait make decisions easily and dislike vacillation, that doesn't necessarily mean they will all make the *same* decisions or the *best* decisions. It just means that they'll make decisions. What each person chooses to do will depend on her values and beliefs. Both Hitler and Mother Teresa can be considered high on Internal Direction.

Internal Direction: The Bad News

Instinctively knowing how to proceed does have a down side: Internally Directed people can have a hard time compromising. If you know what needs to be done and want to go in direction A but your boss wants to go in direction B, you may have a difficult time pursuing course B because you don't believe it is best. And the boss may not be any happier with the situation than you are. If you are not philosophically aligned with those you work for and with, you could be perceived as pushy, stubborn, or not a team player. (Deb created a manual of office procedures. We hope the result was something her boss agreed with.) This is particularly important when more than one person in a group is high on Internal Direction. Since they would all be natural leaders, they need to be philosophically aligned. Otherwise, they will all want to go in different directions.

And it gets worse! Natural leaders usually find followers. If two

> ***Some people follow one leader, while another group
> follows the other. The result can be highly detrimental
> to the organization.***

leaders are not going in the same direction, then factions may be created. Some people follow one leader, while another group follows the other. This is likely to result in an "us vs. them" mentality that can be highly detrimental to the organization.

Remember the Whosits Company, in which the president complained that his vice president always argued direction with him? The president was very upset by this and wanted to fire the vice president. Judi asked whether, before he fired the VP, he would like her to see what the vice president's traits were. That way, the company could avoid hiring a replacement who had the same traits.

It's always essential to consider traits not in isolation but in the context in which they play out. It is wise to look at the traits of the individual and of those he interacts with (boss, subordinates, peers). It's also a good idea to consider the traits that make up the culture of the organization as a whole. When she looked at the VP's writing and the president's writing, Judi found that the president was very strongly Internally Directed. Most of the time he knew what he wanted to do and where he wanted to go. The problem—his VP was just as strongly Internally Directed. Judi told the president,

"You perceive this vice president as not being a team player. He gives you a hard time every time you want to go in a particular direction because he doesn't want to go in the same direction. So he appears stubborn and always seems to want to do his own thing."

The president said, "That's exactly it, and I'm tired of it!"

Judi replied, "Well, you can let him go, but let me explain the trait that is causing the problem behavior." She pointed out how expensive it is to fire and replace someone. Then she explained that the problem was not insubordination but a strong Internal Direction trait. Judi suggested doing a workshop on negotiation skills, and the president agreed. After the president and VP learned how to negotiate common goals, the VP ended up staying.

In this case what was perceived as very negative wasn't really negative. The problem was not that the VP had a strong Internal Direction trait; it was that the president had the same trait, and the two were not always philosophically aligned. In such situations it is important for strongly Internally Directed people to learn negotiating or collaborating skills so they can come up with a compromise or joint direction that all can accept. Once the president and vice president reached agreement on their basic direction, the VP could be left to lead his area of the organization with little or no supervision. And the president could be freed to do other things.

The initial problem in this organization could have been equally difficult if the vice president had not been high on Internal Direction. After all, the president was still strongly Internally Directed, and such individuals tend to think everyone else is like them and expect that others will know what to do next. They may even forget to give clear direction, assuming everyone can read their minds and will know exactly what they think needs to be done. This can create stress among subordinates who need direction—not to mention those who have not yet learned to read minds. . .

When a person high on Internal Direction insists on his way, unlike someone high on Autonomy, it is not because he is ego-invested in the decision and always has to be right. It is because he genuinely believes that his way is the best way. He's committed to a particular approach not because it's *his* approach but because he honestly feels it's the *best* approach.

External Direction: The Good News

The positive side of being Externally Directed is that if you don't have your own agenda and don't know what to do next, you are likely to be willing to listen to those around you—your boss or your team. If they come up with reasonable suggestions, it's likely you'll be willing to go along with them. You'll then be perceived as co-operative and considered to be a team player. Since you don't start out with a strong sense of what course to take, you're not invested in one direction. So you can, if you have other appropriate traits, help others reach consensus. You will also be perceived as fair and objective. You may be considered an exemplary participatory-style or consensus manager. Sounds pretty good, doesn't it? But there is, of course, a hitch.

External Direction: The Bad News

The negative side of being Externally Directed is that without someone to give you direction, you are not able to go forward. You are stuck in neutral or vacillation mode—and this can waste time and money.

Tom, the manufacturing manager of a client company, told Karen, the vice president for operations, that new capital equipment was needed. Karen ordered studies done. Meanwhile, manufacturing was trying to cope with equipment breakdowns. The repair and replacement bills were mounting. "Anything would be better than what we have now!" Tom moaned in despair. A number of options had been presented to Karen, but she always needed a little more time. After all, the purchase represented a major capital expense and she didn't want to be responsible for a costly mistake.

An individual who is not strong on Internal Direction tends to vacillate because she is afraid of making a mistake. Because Karen didn't have the Internal Direction trait, it was extremely difficult for her to make decisions about which of the possibilities should be acted upon. Nor did she have on her executive team a highly Internally Directed person she trusted and could turn to. The result? Karen's delay in making a decision may have cost the company more in repairs and lost production than a poor decision would have.

Fred, who had recently taken over his uncle's failing business, was also Externally Directed. He couldn't make decisions and wasn't sure what to do about the many problems that came to his desk. But he knew how to compensate for that. Fred hired a vice president and certain other team members who were more strongly Internally Directed but did not have other traits that made them controlling. All were collaborative in style. Having chosen the appropriate team, Fred knew how to create an environment in which they could, together, come up with a plan for direction and make decisions. Because they felt included and respected, the team members "bought in" to the decisions that were made. The group became very cohesive and productive. This team turned around a company that was on the brink of bankruptcy.

If You Need Direction

If you are in a leadership position and are not strong on the Internal Direction trait, you need help—either some trusted, strongly Internally Directed people on your team or a mentor to whom you can go for help with decisions. Don't get stuck in the idea that you must do it alone or go only upward for help. Peers, or even those who report to you, may be a rich source of Internal Direction. (One CEO we know goes to his VP of marketing for help in making decisions.) If you haven't made a decision by the end of the day, and the next morning you still can't make one, go to someone who can. Then collaborate until the decision is made. When you delay a decision without a really good reason (say, waiting for important information that will be coming in soon), you are wasting time and money. After all, if the decision were clear and easy, you would have made it immediately—and where's the challenge in that? Remember, most decisions have to get made on less than perfect information.

If you are not in a leadership position and are strongly Externally Directed, you will be happiest in a job in which plenty of direction is available, you have others to help you make a decision in a team atmosphere, or you have clear guidelines about what to do and how to do it. Jobs that require you to follow a system work well for you.

When It Only *Looks* as Though He Knows What to Do

An interesting situation occurs when the boss possesses a high Autonomy trait *in combination with* a high External Direction trait. People high on Autonomy *look* as though they are in charge and know where they are going. No one can tell them what to do. But without much Internal Direction, they desperately need to be told or the organization will be paralyzed. What do you do if you work for such a boss? The first impulse will be to strangle him—but that might not do much for job security. Instead, try presenting him with unfinished ideas. This steers him toward a decision but respects his authority (and his Autonomy trait) by letting him think that all the ideas and decisions were his.

Stagnation vs. Perpetual Conflict: The Corporate Dilemma

The challenge for organizations, of course, is determining what placement will be most productive for each individual. And this is where an understanding of traits can help you make your organization more productive—and less stressful.

Any employee who is not Internally Directed needs someone around who is. Conversely, an individual who is high on the Internal

You don't want a team of all Externally Directed people.
They will never move ahead or get anywhere.

Direction trait performs best when she's not surrounded by others who have the trait to the same degree. So when you put teams together in organizations, you don't want a team in which all the members are strongly Internally Directed; the chances of their all being philosophically aligned are slim. The result will be power struggles as everyone wants to go off in a different direction, and you will lack the cohesiveness essential to productive team dynamics. Nor do you want a team of all Externally Directed people. They will never move ahead or get anywhere. The key is to balance enough Internally Directed team members with others who are Externally Directed.

If you inherit a team with your new position, it is very important to determine what your team's traits are. If your team members are Externally Directed, you'll need to make lists, be available, and give direction when needed. If some team members are strongly Internally Directed, take the time to make sure they're philosophically aligned with you. And if they're *all* strongly Internally Directed, lots of negotiation and discussion will be necessary to come to a

***You don't want a team in which all the members are strongly
Internally Directed; the chances of their all being
philosophically aligned are slim.***

decision that all agree to. This takes more time up front, but then
each player can do his part with little supervision.

Remember Whatsits Inc., the company at which the president
complained to Judi that his vice president couldn't make decisions?
That president, it turned out, was strongly Internally Directed—
and he expected his vice president to be exactly like himself. Since
that wasn't the case, the president thought something was wrong
with his new hire; he wanted the VP to "go back to his office and
make decisions for himself."

Judi said, "That's all well and good, but the reality is that he
doesn't have the Internal Direction trait and *can't* make decisions
easily. When you refuse to tell him what to do, he goes back to his
office and vacillates for three days. That wastes your time and
money. Wouldn't it be easier just to tell him what you want and let
him go back and do it? Once he knows what to do, he can get it done.
He's very good at *doing* things; it's just *figuring out* what to do that's

the problem. If you can point him in the right direction, that would be more productive."

Anyone who possesses a trait to an extreme degree is more likely to encounter problems than someone who has the same trait to a lesser degree. The president would have had a hard time finding someone as strongly Internally Directed as himself who was also perfectly aligned with him philosophically. So the VP who was driving him crazy really wasn't such a bad match after all.

If you are very high on Internal Direction, you can put that trait to use right up front. Use your skills to decide which problem you would rather deal with: having to give extensive directions or having to fight all the time because you are not philosophically aligned with the rest of the team.

Give Advice, Not Direction

There are also people who don't need direction, but do like to get feedback and support for the direction they have chosen. If this describes you, it's important to make it clear to those working with you that you aren't asking for direction, just feedback. (This problem often crops up between spouses when one thinks the other is asking for advice and it's really only feedback that's wanted.) You want to know if the other person thinks this is a good idea or a bad one, but you're not asking for a whole new approach. Needing feedback means you can come up with a direction, and if others were not around, you would go that way. But you also like to hear different perspectives on the goal or direction you've chosen. You like to see if others might come up with ramifications you hadn't considered. This is not a question of "Tell me what to do" but rather "Tell me if what I'm going to do makes sense to you."

In Short

Any trait can be misinterpreted or mishandled. Both Internally Directed and Externally Directed individuals can be successful or

What's the Difference?

	High Internal Direction	Some of Each	High External Direction
Who decides:	self	self and peers	others
Approach to decisions:	confident	varies	much vacillation
Supervision:	unneeded	sometimes needed	necessary unless employee has much experience, follows a routine, or has only limited authority
May appear to be:	headstrong, stubborn, or a natural leader	team player	team player, or indecisive
Problems:	can generate factions, conflict	sometimes needs help with decisions	inability to go forward without direction
Needs:	negotiation skills	occasional clarification of goal	goal clearly stated

unsuccessful on the job; it's the circumstances or team in which each individual is placed that determine that person's success or failure. An Externally Directed person who does exactly what she's told will be a valued employee for a controlling micromanager. If that same employee takes a different job working for a manager who doesn't give clear and consistent direction, she will be extremely *un*successful. The employee is the same; only the circumstances have changed. Being aware of trait differences can allow you to place yourself and others only in successful circumstances.

As simple as these traits seem, it's not immediately obvious which people are highly Internally Directed and which are highly Externally Directed. But by identifying these traits in yourself and in those with whom you deal, you can head off bad placements and

Get It in Writing

To identify an individual's Internal Direction or External Direction trait through handwriting, examine the way that person crosses his T's. The forcefulness of those crossings is a direct indication of how easily he makes decisions. Think of T crossings as the path to the goal.

People high on Internal Direction know where to go and how to get there. They have firm, good-sized T crossings (paths that are easy to see), and most of the crossings do not taper off but have blunt edges.

> *Treating trees* *it the details*
> *lumentation reporting*
> *Tattoo store*

The writing of those with moderate Internal Direction contains a mixture of strong and light or short T crossings. Sometimes these people know where to go; sometimes they don't.

> *that it will turn out* *to the south*
> *interesting, I've sent a copy*
> *not to do the dance*

Those with high External Direction have handwriting in which the T crossings are mostly short and the crossings are light rather than firm (the paths are harder to see). These individuals are not sure where to go, and their T crossings reflect that indecision.

> *best opportunities* *certified graphologist.*
> *home with* *the pictures*

many misunderstandings. In fact, by making sure all the highly Internally Directed people in an organization are generally philosophically aligned and moving in the same direction, you can even avoid the fragmentation that sometimes occurs in an organization as factions are created.

Chapter Five

Structure

A mountain or a molehill?

JACK AND GAIL HAD AN APPOINTMENT for 9:00 A.M. Jack showed up at 9:15. Gail thought, "What an inconsiderate boor. I wonder if he's playing power games with me. We agreed on nine o'clock! How am I going to meet Geoff at 9:30?" She said sweetly, "I thought we had agreed on nine o'clock. I'm afraid I'm going to have to keep this brief."

Jack thought, "What a rigid, uptight person! Gail belongs in the military." He replied, "I didn't realize how tightly scheduled you are. Perhaps you'd rather reschedule."

Structure
Who Are You?

After each question, circle the answer
that comes closest to describing you.

1. I tend to sit in the same seat at the dinner table, conference table, lunchroom table, etc.
a) Always
b) Sometimes
c) Rarely

2. I tend to make lists and then check off the items.
a) All the time
b) Sometimes
c) Lists? What's a list?

3. I'm disappointed when people do not follow through the way they say they will.
a) A lot
b) Occasionally
c) Rarely

4. To me, the method used to reach a goal is just as important as the goal itself.
a) Usually
b) Sometimes
c) Who cares how you get there?

5. When it comes to the details of creating a plan (time, place, when, where, how, who does what, how much, start time, finish time, etc.), I consider myself
a) a very specific planner.
b) a moderately specific planner.
c) someone who plans the goal and figures out the rest as I go.

6. Some people feel it's essential for rules to be consistent for everyone in an organization. I feel that
a) they are absolutely right.
b) most rules should be consistent, but some can be changed.
c) "consistency is the hobgoblin of little minds." Let's go with the flow and apply rules as needed.

7. When someone changes a plan at the last minute, my level of anxiety rises.
a) A lot
b) Some
c) Hey, I'm probably the one who changed it!

8. If someone says he will call me at 2:00 P.M., I plan on talking to that person
a) within five minutes of 2:00 P.M.
b) within half an hour of 2:00 P.M.
c) sometime that afternoon.

9. When I am informed about a new procedure that I will be involved in,
a) it's important for me to have lots of information about how it will be done before I go ahead.
b) I need some information but not a lot.
c) I just do it.

Jack is quite low on the Structure trait, while Gail is quite high. That means that when they interact, misunderstandings are likely to occur. In other words, Jack and Gail are likely to drive each other crazy. Here's why.

People at the high end of the Structure trait continuum tend to form habits easily. They like the familiar and prefer to continue doing what they have been doing. They like to know what to expect. Gail had expected Jack to show up at 9:00 and had organized her day accordingly.

Those at the low end of the Structure trait continuum not only are comfortable with imprecision and change; they actually *need* flexibility and freedom. They find it uncomfortable to follow the agendas that those at the high end of the Structure trait like to create. Jack never imagined that 15 minutes could make such a difference.

Climbing the Mountain of Anxiety

The only way to make a change is to do what is unfamiliar and uncomfortable. For those high on the Structure trait, going from the

---

10. When asked to change one of my systems, I feel
a) a lot of anxiety.
b) moderate anxiety.
c) little anxiety.

SCORING
Add up your total score, using the following values for your answers.

1.	a) 5	b) 3	c) 0	3.	a) 5	b) 2	c) 0	
2.	a) 5	b) 2	c) 0	4.	a) 5	b) 3	c) 0	
				5.	a) 5	b) 3	c) 0	
				6.	a) 5	b) 2	c) 0	
				7.	a) 5	b) 3	c) 0	
				8.	a) 5	b) 2	c) 0	
				9.	a) 5	b) 2	c) 0	
				10.	a) 5	b) 3	c) 0	

If your score is between 0 and 15, you're low on the Structure trait. A score of 16 to 35 indicates moderate Structure, and a score of 36 or higher means you're high on Structure.

---

familiar to the unfamiliar or new is like climbing a mountain of anxiety. For high Structure people to change what they are used to means they can't do what grounds them, and they are not grounded in the new context. So the period in between is a tense one.

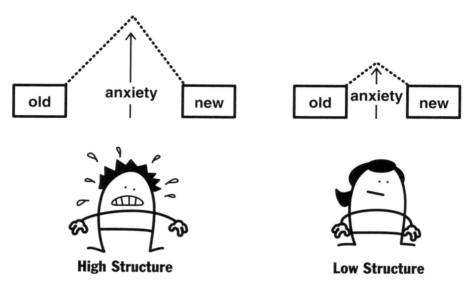

High Structure   **Low Structure**

For a person with a high Structure trait (left), going from the familiar to the unfamiliar is like climbing a mountain of anxiety. The low Structure person (right) takes change in stride.

It is this period—the time immediately surrounding a change—that we have named "the mountain of anxiety." This "mountain" has two sides, each associated with distinct behaviors. And as any mountain climber knows, while it's a challenge to get up the mountain, getting down isn't always a piece of cake either.

Resistance: "We Can't Do That!"

The first side of the mountain is called the resistance phase. Judi was consulted by a couple in which the husband, Brian, scored low on Structure, but his wife, Tobi, was high on Structure. They were working in the backyard one day when Brian said, "I think we need more sun on the house. I'll cut down some trees."

Cutting down trees meant change, so Tobi's immediate response was, "Don't cut down any trees! We really need these trees. They're good for the ecology, they shade the house, and they look so nice!" This is typical high Structure behavior, giving every objection to the change and every reason to maintain the status quo (on the resistance side of the mountain).

When a company hands down a change, usually the first thing heard is grumbling. It's not that people don't want to be team players or aren't committed to the company; it has nothing to do with that. The resistance phase is automatic and instinctual. It's due to the Structure trait. People need time to climb that side of the mountain of anxiety, and they need time to complain about it. They need time to get beyond their anxieties, which will be presented in the form of objections. They need to know why the proposed change is good or beneficial in order to scale the resistance side of the mountain.

In the case of Tobi and Brian, Brian was used to Tobi's reactions to proposed changes. So he kept raking the leaves while she was in the long resistance phase. Then every once in a while, he would interject something like, "We'll have less mold in the house," or "We'll use less heating oil in the winter."

Adjustment: "How Would We Do That?"

If you give high Structure people enough reasons why a particular change really is a good move, then they "peak the mountain" and start to display a second behavior, the behavior of emotional adjustment. It's at this point that they start to fill in the details. They need to get comfortable with the idea and feel that they know what to expect. When they have worked out enough details so that they can anticipate how things will work, their comfort level increases and they become less anxious.

The high Structure person must work out the details to get used to a new idea. Then, and only then, can he actually make the move.

Of course, he might come back two weeks later and say, "We should have done this years ago." And that might be true—but years ago he still would have had to climb that mountain.

It's important to recognize that the size of the mountain depends on two things: the extent of the proposed change and the strength of the individual's Structure trait. If the change is a major one (e.g., changing the direction of the company, as opposed to moving offices to a different floor) and the person is high on the Structure trait, both the resistance and adjustment phases will take some time.

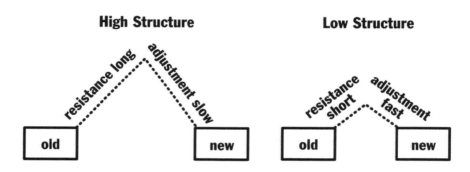

If you give high Structure people enough reasons why a particular change really is a good move, then they "peak the mountain" and start to display a second behavior, the behavior of emotional adjustment. For low Structure people, the process is much faster.

Bumps, Hills, and Mountains

If the person is low on Structure, then the phases will be very short. People low on the Structure trait don't have a lot of stress around change. They experience a small, short bump rather than a mountain of anxiety. It doesn't take much time to get over it. These people have fewer objections and need fewer details to get comfortable with the planned change.

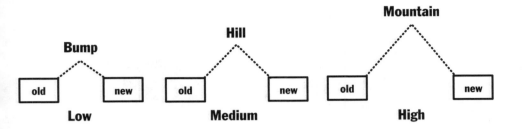

Depending on a person's Structure trait, the amount of time needed to adjust to change varies.

Those in the middle on the Structure trait will have hills to climb. They may grumble publicly or privately, and they will need to understand some reasons for the change and some of the details of it. They will be able to accept change more quickly than high Structure people, but less quickly than low Structure people.

When an individual proposes a change himself, he has already climbed the mountain, hill, or bump of anxiety in his own mind, so resistance and adjustment are no longer issues. Barbara was a high Structure person, and her coworkers had come to expect consistency from her. They were shocked one morning when she showed up at work with a hairstyle radically different from the one they had seen for years. When her friend Jean remarked on the sudden change, Barbara revealed that she had been discussing this new look with her hairdresser for the past six months. Once she was sure of how it would look and how she would maintain it, she made the change. It really was not a sudden move at all. Barbara had actually climbed a very large, hairy mountain.

But when change comes *to* the individual rather than *from* her, we can expect certain behaviors, depending on the strength of her Structure trait. The Structure trait does not tell if people *will* change,

When her friend Jean remarked on the sudden change, Barbara revealed that she had been discussing this new look with her hairdresser for the past six months.

only how they will go through the change, how long it may take them, and how much anxiety they will feel in the process.

The Enlargeable/Shrinkable Frame

Once Tobi voiced all her objections about cutting down the trees, she had scaled the mountain of anxiety. Then she started the adjustment phase—the other side of the mountain of anxiety. Because her mountain was high, she needed a lot of detailed information to get comfortable. So she said, "If we're going to cut down some trees, which ones will we take down?"

Anyone familiar with traits would not be surprised by this question. High Structure people like to know exactly what to expect. Low Structure people like flexibility and see everything as approximate. For them it's not only acceptable but desirable to "work it out as we go."

Remember, Brian's initial statement was "I think I'll cut down some trees." It is not unusual for low Structure people to speak in generalities: "We'll do it soon." "It'll take a while." "We'll need a few people." They haven't thought about particulars because they are comfortable before they fill in the details. Brian just said he would cut down some trees. How many? Which trees? When would they be cut? He didn't worry about those pieces because he didn't need that much information to feel comfortable with the idea.

When Tobi asked, "Which trees?" Brian replied, "We'll take some trees down on this side of the house." Low Structure Brian speaks in generalities or "broad frames." Anything in the frame is okay with him. People like high Structure Tobi try to shrink the frame—getting low Structure Brian to be more specific. "Some on this side" was a little more specific, but it was still too broad a frame for high Structure Tobi.

It took some time, but Tobi finally got Brian to shrink the frame considerably. They put ribbons around four trees to be cut down, called stump-removal companies for estimates, hired a company to come at a specific time, and figured out what to do with the wood and where to put the wood

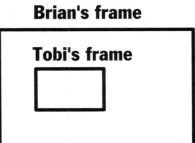

chips. At last, Tobi was comfortable and could accept the change. She knew exactly what would happen and what to expect. All the particulars were filled in, and the steps down the adjustment side of the mountain were complete. She told Brian to go ahead while she ran some errands. And that, from her rueful point of view when she returned, was where she made her mistake. . .

When a high Structure person leaves the discussion table, she views the frame she has accepted as being carved in stone. And it's not just the *end* that is, in her mind, unchangeable; it's the means of getting there too. So far as the high Structure person is concerned, the unspoken agreement is that "this is what I expect and the way I expect it to be accomplished." For the high Structure person, the way the goal is reached (the means) is as important as the end result. Anything outside the agreed-upon frame is inappropriate and unacceptable.

For a low Structure person, on the other hand, all decisions are firmly carved in pudding. No matter how specific the debate, when he leaves the decision table, the low Structure person automatically and instinctively moves the frame back to its original broad size— i.e., "I'll cut down some trees to get more sun." From *his* point of view, anything within that original frame is acceptable. What he cares about is the end, not the means. In that large frame, any number of trees is okay, and any selection of specific trees is reasonable.

When two people have such dramatically different preconceptions of what's acceptable, it's not surprising that somebody will find the outcome entirely *un*acceptable. And that's what happened in this case. When Brian went to cut down the four trees, he suddenly realized that the sun is at a different angle in winter than in summer, and if they cut down the chosen trees, they wouldn't get the additional sun they wanted in the winter. Brian was a caring, conscientious person, and he wanted to do the best he could. The way he saw it, it wouldn't make any sense to cut down the particular trees he and Tobi had identified, given the goal of getting more sun. It would be much better to take five *different* trees. And that's exactly what he proceeded to do.

Tobi returned to see the four beribboned trees standing, but five other trees cut down. She exploded. "I can never trust you unless I watch you every minute!" she shrieked. "You are unreliable and you lie to me!"

He, of course, assumed she was like him in that all she wanted was to get more sun. "But I *told* you I was going to cut down some trees," he protested. Tobi thought that Brian was unreliable and didn't care about her needs, and Brian thought Tobi was uptight and rigid. They blamed each other for their problems and came to Judi for a consultation.

Tobi and Brian's dilemma was not unusual. When two or more people agree on a decision and walk away from the discussion table, each assumes his expectations will be met. For the high Structure person, that means that everything will take place exactly as agreed upon. If things don't evolve in exactly the way she's been led to anticipate, she is very disappointed and concludes that others are not reliable. The low Structure person, on the other hand, looks at life—and decisions—very differently. For that individual, both the agreed-upon goal and the means to it can be revised as the work progresses.

All Brian and Tobi needed was to understand the Structure trait and their very different places on the Structure continuum. Once that was clarified, Tobi understood that Brian did care about her needs. And he understood that, in order to alleviate her anxiety, he needed to inform Tobi in advance of what seemed to him to be trivial changes.

Frames in the Office: "That's Not My Job!"

Exactly the same principles apply in the workplace. Suppose a high Structure manager agrees with a low Structure manager to spend a million dollars on project X. When they leave the discussion table, the high Structure manager's picture of project X is limited to a frame of a million dollars. But when the low Structure manager leaves the table, the frame automatically expands in her mind. Instead of exactly a million dollars, she thinks of it as "somewhere in the neighborhood of a million dollars." For low Structure people, everything is a range. They hate to be pinned down. They like flexibility.

If a low Structure manager asks a high Structure employee to do something outside his job description (the frame), the high Structure employee will look at her very seriously and say, "But that's not my job." He will be on the resistance side of his mountain. To the high Structure employee, this new request is not in the frame he agreed to. In order to do something outside his frame, he has to go through both the resistance phase and an emotional adjustment phase—all of which can strike the low Structure manager as just a bit much.

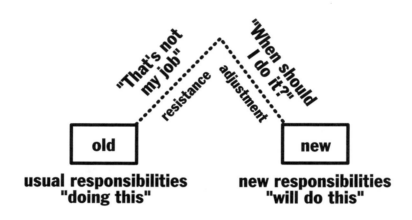

old
usual responsibilities
"doing this"

new
new responsibilities
"will do this"

To the high Structure employee, a request to handle new duties is not in the frame he agreed to.

The low Structure manager immediately concludes, "He's not a team player. He doesn't care about the company. He's not adaptable. He's not cooperative." She may not say these things, but there's no doubt that's what she's thinking. What she has asked is not, to her, a big deal. But to a high Structure person, any change is a big deal and requires time in which to adjust.

Of course, a low Structure employee who sees something outside his job description that needs to be done will do it. And if he has a high Structure manager, the manager may say, "Why are you doing that? That's not your job!" Maybe it's true that no good deed goes unpunished. . .

You Can Set Your Watch by Him

Since high Structure people want to know what to expect, predictability and consistency are very important to them. Consider the high Structure employee in one of Judi's client companies. This employee had worked for the same company for 21 years, and for 21 years, he'd arrived at work every day within three minutes of 7:00 A.M. That kind of consistency is typical of someone with a high Structure trait. A high Structure individual tends to form habits because habits make his life predictable. The higher a person's Structure trait, the more tightly that person will keep to his habits. Twenty-one years of arriving at work within three minutes of 7:00 suggest that this individual was about as high on Structure as you can get. If he hadn't arrived by 7:05, you knew something was wrong. But if you wanted to hold a meeting at 7:05, you could count on him to be there.

Consistency is wonderful in some situations—it's essential for a copy editor or a quality-control manager. But at other times, when change is required, it can be problematic.

David, the CEO of one of Judi's client companies, arranged a seminar for his executive team and announced that it would start at 8:00 in the morning. By 7:55, everyone had assembled—except David. He didn't arrive until 8:25. David was high in Structure, and his habit was to arrive at work each day at 8:25. Even though he had himself set the seminar for 8:00, he was unable to break his normal routine and get there early. The members of his team all laughed. They could always set their watches by him, so they had never really expected him before 8:25.

Another high Structure client, Jenn, told us of a problem she was having with her new job. Although the job started at 8:00, Jenn never managed to arrive before 8:20, no matter how hard she tried. She knew this was not making a good impression on her boss—and she didn't blame him. Accountability and reliability were very important to her; she was used to sticking to agreements to the letter. Yet, she had agreed to start her job at 8:00 A.M. and found herself arriving at 8:20! She couldn't understand why she was having so much difficulty.

When Jenn came for a consultation, Judi asked her what time her previous job had started. Eight-thirty, Jenn said. What time had she arrived at work each day for the previous job? Eight-twenty. Jenn

Jenn had formed a habit, and as a high Structure person, she was having a hard time breaking it.

had formed a habit, and as a high Structure person, she was having a hard time breaking it. Her values and intentions weren't enough to overcome that ingrained habit quickly. In her prior job, her trait behavior had been an asset, and she was viewed as reliable, dependable, and committed—all characteristics she valued. In the current job, the exact same trait behavior resulted in giving people exactly the opposite impression! Every trait has its advantages and disadvantages, depending upon the situation. However, once Jenn realized what was going on, she was able to break her habit. Awareness of traits allows us to make choices about our behavior.

Other traits may be involved in how a person reacts to change. But only a person who is high on the Structure trait will generally be reluctant to accept change at first. And only someone who is high on Structure will consistently go through a process of resistance and emotional adjustment before finally accepting any change.

Dealing with High Structure People

How do you handle a high Structure person in the workplace? There are several ways you can make everyone more comfortable.

Allow Time for Climbing

First, give plenty of time for the resistance phase, without being judgmental. This allows the high Structure person a chance to vent objections and scale the first side of that mountain of anxiety. Don't expect instant acceptance. Give valid reasons for the change and wait for her to make it over the mountain.

If you're patient, the employee will move on from resistance to the emotional adjustment phase. That's when she will begin to ask the how, when, and where questions. Take the time to fill in these answers, and be sure to provide detail in proportion to the size of the mountain you are dealing with. This entire process will feel like it takes a bit longer than you'd like, but it's important to allow time for it. If you don't, the high Structure person will never accept the change. You may be able to force the individual into the new situation, but unless you allow time for her to deal with it, she won't be happy—and neither will you.

Sara asked her high Structure employee, Jeff, to handle the front desk one day because the receptionist was out sick. Jeff immediately went into resistance mode. "That's not my job," he told Sara. "I have too much work to do. I'll fall behind. Besides, I'm not comfortable handling customers."

If Sara hadn't been aware of Jeff's high Structure trait, she might have viewed him as argumentative, uncommitted, and not a team player. Fortunately, Sara recognized the trait, and she patiently addressed his concerns. He was right, she told him; it wasn't in his job description. But this was an emergency. He could delay his own work, and she didn't expect him to be perfect at handling customers. Understanding all this, Jeff then reached the summit of the mountain and began the adjustment phase, discussing how he could stay late tomorrow to finish his own work and whom he could ask for help in dealing with customers. Because Sara maintained a nonjudgmental attitude toward Jeff and allowed him time to climb the mountain of anxiety, the episode actually enhanced their working relationship.

Give Advance Notice

High Structure people need to be informed in advance of all changes—even those that may appear to a lower Structure person to be trivial. They need to be told the reason for each change, too. If this is not done, the high Structure person can feel insecure; after all, if he doesn't know what to expect, he can't plan for it.

And what if the move is a positive one? The reaction is likely to be the same. Even something others view as a positive change can seem negative to a high Structure person, just because it's change.

Tim, a high Structure manager, asked his lower Structure subordinate Kassi when she could submit the sum total of past-due accounts. Kassi said she could get it to him on Friday. Tim, of course, asked, "*When* on Friday?" Kassi said midday. Not surprisingly, the next question was, "What time?" She replied it would be ready at noon. Tim planned to order lunch in and go over the document with her at lunch, calculating that he had a meeting at eleven and another at one o'clock and had just enough time in between to deal with the report.

Kassi finished the report early, at ten o'clock on Friday. She thought, "Tim will be pleased to see that I've gotten this done early! I'll take it to him now." She brought it in and put it on his desk. But instead of the praise she expected, she got an annoyed, "Take it away. I'll look at it at noon." She walked away disappointed, confused, and upset at his response. Kassi had thought she was being efficient by getting the report in early, but he had perceived the early delivery as an interference in his planned schedule.

Once a high Structure person has an understanding of what will happen, he organizes his time around it. Tim had planned his day so that he could look at the report at noon. The early report was a change that interfered with his plan for the day. High Structure people get disappointed in those who do not follow through within the tight frame of their expectations, so it is very important to make sure they know about modifications ahead of time. Had Kassi called Tim in the morning to tell him she could get the report to him by ten, he could have told her he couldn't meet with her until noon. Or he could have modified his schedule to meet with her. In either case, the early notice would have prevented his annoyance.

If a high Structure person has time to adjust, he can climb the mountain. When dealing with such an employee or boss, provide plenty of lead time on changes, and give advance notice of even those changes that seem inconsequential to you, such as having a report ready two hours early. This approach is essential to maintaining good relationships with high Structure people.

It's particularly important for anyone being hired for a new job to know whether the prospective boss is high or low on Structure. A high Structure boss will want exactly what he tells you he wants with regard to product, process, and timing. He will be disappointed if you do not give him what he expects in the way he expects it.

The high Structure prospective employee also wants to know what to expect. In the case of the employee, this translates to a job description that's laid out precisely. The employee will want to know exactly when reviews will occur, and when and how much her raises will be. If a high Structure person is told that she'll be reviewed on her six-month anniversary, that is when she expects to be reviewed—not a week earlier or a month later. If the high Structure person's expectations around these issues are not met, she may feel her boss is untrustworthy or unreliable.

Dealing with Low Structure People

An individual who's low on Structure has a frame of expectation for her job that's wide and nonspecific; she's likely to view it in terms of "helping the company" or "working a full day." She won't be upset if her job description is vague because the details aren't what's important to her. In fact, she doesn't much care what *anybody's* job description is. When a person with a low Structure trait sees something that needs to be done, she might walk over and do it; she reasons that she is paid for an eight-hour day and that she should do anything she can to help.

Don't Assume Negative Intentions

But that's not how things look to the high Structure person, who's more likely to view such "helpfulness" as butting in. To the high Structure person, whose frame of expectation is narrow and specific, the person low on Structure is doing something outside the acceptable frame. To say that friction can result is putting it politely. This is why it is important to know whether your coworkers are high or low on the Structure trait.

Expect Change

Remember that people low on this trait do not form habits. A lower Structure employee may arrive at work at a different time every day. One day he may come in at seven o'clock, another at nine. If you want to have a meeting at 7:30, you can't assume that person will be in the office unless you inform him ahead of time that the meeting will start at exactly 7:30. And if a 7:30 meeting is *scheduled* by someone who's low on the Structure trait, remember that that person's frame is wide; unless he values punctuality, the meeting could start as early as seven or as late as eight o'clock. Clear your calendar for the morning!

If your boss is low on Structure, your job may end up being very different from what you were led to expect initially. Keep in mind that this kind of boss deals within very large (and vague) frames of expectation. There probably won't be a detailed job description—

at least not one created by the boss. Instead, the (unwritten) job description could turn into anything the boss thinks needs to be done. Or there may be a written job description that's very broad, and you'll be expected to develop it. The subordinate never knows exactly what's expected. And if he does figure it out? Well, by the next day, the boss's ideas of what's needed may have changed anyway.

The solution? You won't be able to change this boss's (or coworker's) changeable nature. But you *can* manage how you deal with it. Plan for maximum flexibility, put goals and directions in writing, and recognize that expectations are likely to change along the way.

Make Him Write It Down

Paige was a graduate student at a prestigious business school. She was smart and talented; her company, recognizing this, was footing the bill so she could take time off and earn her MBA through a high-powered one-year executive MBA program. Paige also had a high Structure trait. Once she adjusted to the new school's environment and got into the routine, she was meeting or exceeding all the requirements of her program. Then she was assigned an adviser.

Paige met with Ray, her adviser, and he told her what was needed in order for her final project to be approved. Paige followed his instructions to the letter, doing a stellar job. At the next meeting she confidently presented her work, knowing she had met all the requirements. She was shocked when Ray told her that she now had to meet *further* requirements, and that some of what she'd already done was not necessary. It seemed like a bad dream.

This happened three times. Paige wondered if Ray was playing power games. Or maybe he was forgetful. Or maybe—this was beginning to seem pretty likely—he was just plain crazy. She came to Judi quite frazzled and discouraged. She was running out of time before the end of the school year, and she couldn't seem to satisfy her adviser.

When Judi saw a sample of Ray's handwriting, she noticed that he was very low on the Structure trait. Remember, people low on this trait find change easy, so they assume it is easy for everyone. What had seemed to Paige an exact agreement on the requirements had to him been only an approximate agreement. Low Structure people tend to expand the frame after a high Structure person thinks everything has been settled. It was natural for Ray to then refer to any or all aspects of the broad frame, while Paige referenced only those aspects of the frame that had been agreed upon specifically.

Judi explained that Ray was not forgetful or crazy, and he wasn't playing power games; he simply had a low Structure trait. Judi knew that Ray would change the requirements yet again—but she proposed a solution. This time Paige was to write down the new assignment immediately and give a copy to Ray before proceeding; she was to ask him whether the assignment was described correctly and whether, if she followed it to the letter, that would result in approval of her project. Paige followed Judi's suggestion and Ray said yes, the new description accurately represented what was needed.

When she completed the assignment, Paige presented her project once again. And again Ray started to change the requirements. But this time Paige showed him the written agreement from their previous meeting. He had no choice but to approve her project.

Structure and Organizations

The Structure trait also can be seen in the overall culture of an organization. If a particular company is high on Structure, then benefits will be awarded consistently to all employees, and boundaries, systems, procedures, policies, practices, etc. will all be laid out clearly. Employees of the high Structure manager will know whether they measure up and exactly where they fall short. The high Structure employee will find this clarity helpful; the low Structure employee may find it stifling. A low Structure employee working for a high Structure company may do best out on the road (perhaps in a sales position), with the ability to set his own schedule.

When Ray started to change the requirements, Paige showed him the written agreement from their previous meeting. He had no choice but to approve her project.

In a low Structure culture, not as much will be laid out precisely. Some employees may get certain benefits, while others receive different ones. There may not be much consistency. In low Structure companies, employees wear many hats, and there are no clear boundaries between jobs. Job descriptions are vague or nonexistent. Low Structure employees of such companies appreciate the versatility and flexibility afforded by such an environment; their high Structure coworkers are likely to feel anxious or angry at the lack of consistency. Accountants can function in low Structure companies because they can create structure within their own departments. Usually low Structure people appreciate seeing their paychecks come consistently and are willing to support structure in that area.

Obviously, the middle of the continuum offers both flexibility and some consistency—so some employees at each end of the Structure spectrum will be happy and some discontented. The critical factor here is that each company's culture is established by those who run the company. If a new leader steps in, the culture could change to reflect the new leader's traits.

What's the Difference?

	High Structure	Low Structure
Needs:	predictability and consistency	flexibility and freedom
Communicates:	with specifics and details	in generalities
Reacts to change with:	immediate negativity, anxiety. Needs much information to ease adjustment	interest. Rest of reaction depends on specifics
Sees those with opposite trait as:	unreliable or dishonest, butting into areas not assigned them	rigid, tense, picky; not team players; not willing to help out
Shows in organizations through:	policies, systems, procedures laid out and rule-driven	policies, systems, procedures not standardized; much flexibility

In Short

It's not unusual for someone to be accused of being unfair, picky, lazy, or rigid when in fact that person is simply high on the Structure trait. Similarly, people who are low on the Structure trait are often described as dishonest, unreliable, or unfair; they're accused of changing the rules in mid game.

The degree to which each individual possesses the Structure trait tells us the degree to which that person will experience anxiety when confronted with change. This trait does not indicate *if* a person will change, but *how* the person will change and what he will experience when confronted with a new situation. Structure also indicates how people plan; it determines how much detail they need in order to proceed and how closely they expect the details of

Get It in Writing

High Structure people are consistent, and their writing shows consistency in the slant, size, and flow of the writing.

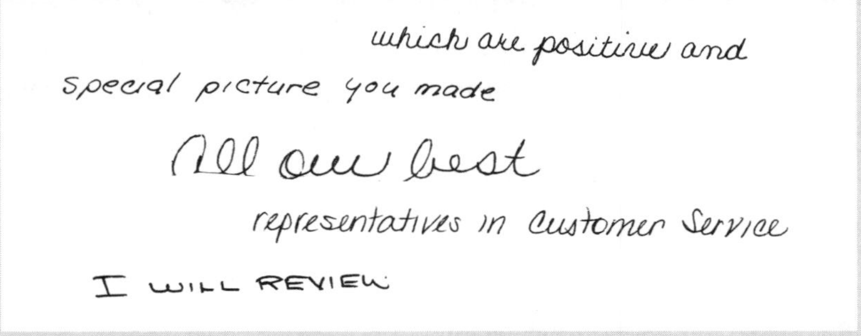

> which are positive and
> special picture you made
> All our best
> representatives in Customer Service
> I WILL REVIEW

The handwriting of someone with moderate Structure shows some flexibility and less consistency than that of the high Structure person, but still shows some flow and consistency.

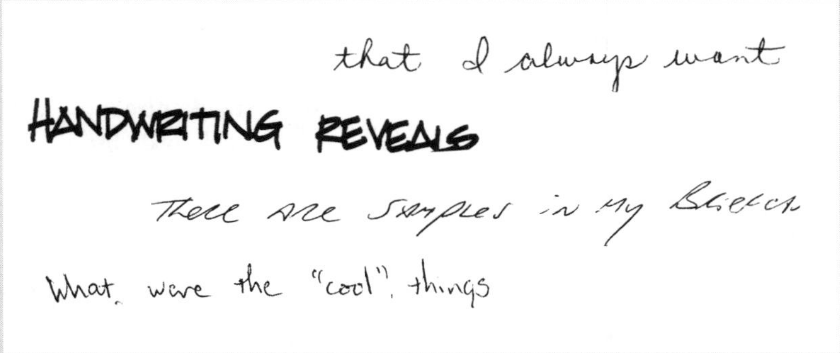

> that I always want
> HANDWRITING REVEALS
> There are samples in my Sketch
> What were the "cool" things

The writing of someone with low Structure shows an unpredictable mixture of slant and letter size.

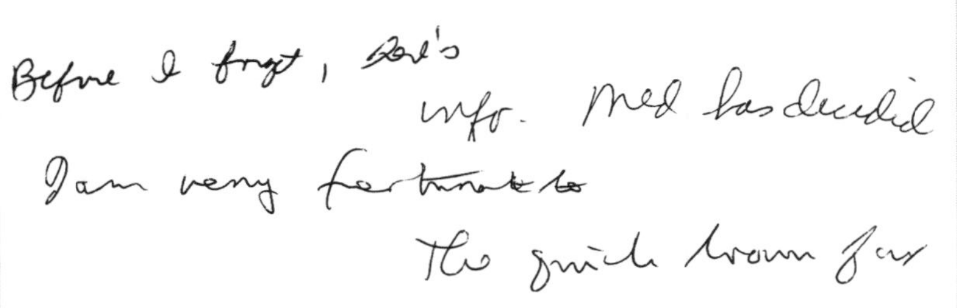

> Before I forgt, here's
> info. Med has decided
> I am very fortunate to
> The quick brown fox

the plan to be adhered to.

As with all traits, what gets people into trouble is the belief that "everyone is like me, needs what I need, and expects what I expect." What can alleviate such problems is an awareness of the Structure trait and how those who possess the trait to varying degrees will automatically and instinctively react. With awareness comes understanding, and with understanding comes a greater opportunity to be supportive rather than critical of each other.

Chapter Six

Conventional and Alternative

Where did that *idea come from?*

B
OB AND ANDREA WERE IN CHARGE of planning a restaurant dinner for an important client. Bob suggested a local gourmet restaurant. Andrea said, "Why don't we hold the dinner at the plant? It could be a moving dinner—the appetizers in one division, soup in another, and so on. That way, we could show off the plant at the same time."

Bob responded, "Andrea, we're supposed to pick out a restaurant.

Conventional and Alternative
Who Are You?

After each question, circle the answer
that comes closest to describing you.

1. People accuse me of not addressing the question at hand or of getting totally off track.
a) Rarely
b) Occasionally
c) How did you know?

2. I find myself using objects for purposes for which they were never intended.
a) Often
b) Occasionally
c) Huh?

3. I instinctively use similar methods over and over to solve a problem—even when it looks as if they're not working.
a) Usually
b) Occasionally
c) No way!

4. Others view my ideas as unusual or far out.
a) Frequently
b) Sometimes
c) Never

5. When presented with a new idea, my first response is to ask
a) how it would work.
b) for more information.
c) what else could be done.

6. When confronted with a problem of decreasing business revenues,
a) I typically look for ways to cut costs and increase efficiencies.
b) my reaction depends on the circumstances.
c) I'm likely to look for new products or new uses or markets for existing products.

7. If I weren't selling enough of a certain book in my store, I would
a) try to display the copies better and advertise more.
b) write them off as a loss.
c) pile them up and use them as display pedestals.

SCORING
Add up your total score, using the following values for your answers.

1.	a) 0	b) 3	c) 5
2.	a) 5	b) 3	c) 0
3.	a) 0	b) 3	c) 5
4.	a) 5	b) 3	c) 0
5.	a) 0	b) 3	c) 5
6.	a) 0	b) 3	c) 5
7.	a) 0	b) 0	c) 5

A score from 0 through 10 indicates a Conventional trait. Anything from 11 through 25 suggests that you possess some of both traits, and a score of 26 or higher means you have more of the Alternative trait.

That is what we were told to do. These people have been our clients for five years, and we've taken them to dinner at a restaurant every one of those years. If we do something this different, the clients will think we're weird, and we could lose their respect. Who ever heard of a moving dinner anyway?"

Andrea replied, "We don't have to do the traditional thing. Let's think of what else we can do instead. That might be more interesting."

The Conventional and Alternative traits tell us how people think. People with either of these traits can be "creative," but the source and nature of their creativity differs. Understanding these traits can be critical to the success or failure of individuals and companies.

Thinking in the Box vs. Out of the Box

When an idea is mentioned, a person with the Conventional trait will automatically and instinctively begin to talk (if verbal) or think (if nonverbal) within the idea; he'll work "in the box." Suppose the idea is "Let's buy a new house." The Conventional person will tend to stay within the boundaries of the stated idea (buying a new house) and try to figure out the best way to do that. He will consider such things as neighborhood, financing, size, schools, interest rates, etc., all geared to determining the feasibility and practicality of the idea of buying a new house. We call this "thinking into the idea." Conventional people are concerned with how to do things; they try to do things better, faster, more smoothly, and more creatively than they were done before. Alternative people instinctively ask what else can be done. They look for ideas that are different from the original one.

Because Bob had the Conventional trait and the original assignment was to have dinner at a restaurant, he wanted to develop a practical, feasible plan around doing just that. But for Andrea, who had the Alternative trait, the natural reaction was entirely different. Instead of thinking *into* the idea, Alternative people think *away*

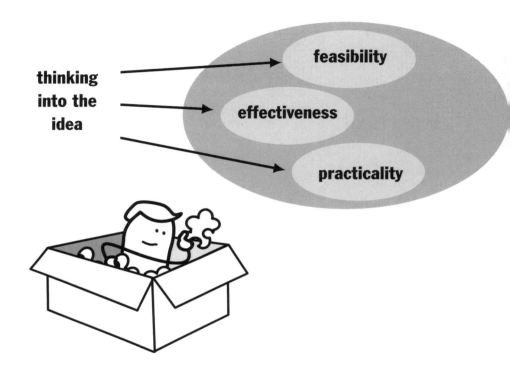

A person with the Conventional trait will automatically and instinctively begin to talk or think within the idea; he'll work "in the box."

from it; they instinctively try to figure out what can be done instead of the original proposal. Andrea automatically and instinctively thought about something *other* than having dinner at a restaurant.

The person with the Alternative trait will think or talk about other possibilities that were not part of the original idea. If everyone is pointing in one direction, she will automatically look the other way, instinctively substituting something else for whatever was suggested. Alternative people can be considered irritating when they appear to

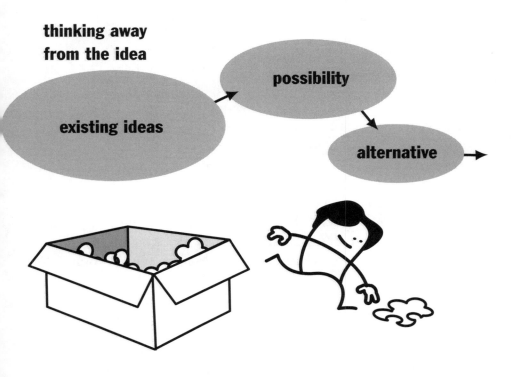

thinking away from the idea

existing ideas

possibility

alternative

The person with the Alternative trait will think or talk about other possibilities that were not part of the original idea; he'll work "out of the box."

immediately change the subject—a characteristic that is often perceived at best as getting off the track or away from the topic. They may be considered flighty or ungrounded. And let's face it: to a Conventional person, they can be downright frustrating.

Why Conventional People Need to Get Out More

Conventional people get ideas from existing ideas. These are ideas they may have read about, seen on TV or in other companies, learned in seminars, or heard about from friends. Seeing or hearing about an existing idea or product gives them food for thought. Then they instinctively begin to improve on the idea or sometimes combine two existing ideas to create something new. The Conventional person sees razor-blade holders in a variety of colors and thinks, "I bet our widget holders would sell better in colors, too." Conventional people need to expose themselves to a broad range of activities to stimulate their creativity. The more Conventional people are exposed to existing ideas, the more material they have to work from, and the more creative they can be.

Most high-fashion clothes are based on the designers' experiences viewing period costumes in museums, paying close attention to the wardrobes used in movies, or checking out the latest street styles. Some even have scouts out looking at what young Al-

When two or more of these Conventional people come together, as they might in a team setting, they begin to share their "sacks of ideas" with each other.

ternative trendsetters are wearing. They gather all their ideas from these sources and put them together in creative ways, perhaps using unusual new materials for traditional styles or combining already-popular looks in new ways.

As a Conventional person moves through life, he accumulates ideas. All the people, places, and situations he experiences contribute to what we call the "sack of ideas" that he carries along with him. Each new situation, idea, or learning experience adds a new element—sometimes a whole bunch of them—to the collection of ideas in the sack. When two or more of these Conventional people come together, as they might in a team setting, they begin to share their ideas and empty their sacks for each other.

In the beginning, this is very exciting because the Conventional members of the team get to see what is in all the sacks, and each person gets to add to his own collection. Everyone's sack gets bigger, and there is plenty of food for thought. The result? The team is, for a while, very creative.

Eventually, though, the group reaches a point at which all the sacks have been emptied and their contents shared and played with. There are no ideas left that have not been seen. Since they haven't anything novel to share, the Conventional members then begin to reuse the same old ideas over and over. The team becomes stale, flat, less and less creative—in short: boring. That is usually the point at which a company will say, "We need new blood." It is not necessarily new blood that's needed; it's new sacks—or new additions to the old sacks.

An Owner's Guide to the Conventional Trait

People with the Conventional trait need to constantly refill their sacks by exposing themselves to ideas; they can do this by attending trade shows, reading lots of books and magazines, taking classes, talking with other people, or going to new places. Because the Conventional person derives his ideas from the world and the ideas that exist in it, it's very important for him to keep up that constant exposure to existing ideas. When the Conventional person isolates himself or limits his exposure and range of interests, he automatically limits his potential ideas and creativity. Without outside ideas, he has no source of inspiration—no food for thought. He ends up reusing the same old ideas again and again.

In private life, too, the Conventional person will try to improve upon an existing idea even when a whole new approach is needed. The Conventional spouse may nag her husband to pick up his mess. When that doesn't work, she will try nagging louder, more frequently, or by other means—she might leave notes about the offending behavior, or try to get the kids to nag, too. But all this is still nagging. So what can you do? If you're a Conventional thinker, you've used up all the ideas in your sack, and the problem still is not resolved, then it is time to find an Alternative thinker who understands your goal and can figure out a nontraditional way to reach it.

The Conventional person can't always find the right idea himself. There's nothing wrong with that; it is perfectly all right to seek out people known for unusual approaches and to be open to something entirely different. Sometimes this is called desperation. Take the case of Joanne and Steve, whose five-year-old daughter, Kara, had bitten her nails so severely that her parents worried about deformity. They had tried every conventional approach— punishments ranging from time-outs to withholding television and candy—and had taken her to the pediatrician for some foul-tasting nail paint. They were demonstrating instinctive Conventional behavior: trying to stop the problem. But none of these negative approaches to the nail biting worked. Finally Joanne read an article about treating the problem in an entirely different way. Following the approach explained in the article, Joanne ordered Kara to bite her nails at frequent, specific times of day. Very soon, Kara was complaining when ordered to bite her nails and stopped biting them on her own. Instead of trying to stop

Finally Joanne read an article that led her to treating Kara's nail-biting problem in an entirely different way.

the problem directly, this Alternative approach succeeded by *demanding* the behavior.

Stranded on a Desert Island? Better Hope You're with an Alternative Thinker

Alternative thinkers' ideas come from inside them. Even locked in a tower or stranded on a desert island, the Alternative thinker's creativity would be unimpaired because she is not restricted by what is in her invisible sack (her experiences). Sir Isaac Newton certainly was not the first person who ever had an apple fall on his head—but when it happened to him, he wondered why. And then he came up with a concept that no one had considered before: gravity. Clearly this was not something he had seen, since it is invisible, nor had he (to our knowledge) read about it. He came up with a name and an explanation for something everyone had noticed, but no one had ever named or tried to explain.

Why Alternative Thinking Kids Need Fewer Toys

Conventional thinkers work from existing ideas and usually work within the original intent of the object or idea. A Conventional thinker might come up with the idea of making a radio waterproof, for example, so it can be put into the shower. Its purpose is still entertainment. People with the Alternative trait, too, can create new things from what already exists. However, they use the existing objects and ideas in ways that were never originally intended. A Conventional thinker would see bean-bag toys and think about making them in new, improved colors, fabrics, and sizes. An Alternative thinker would make them into chairs. Alternative thinking kids always figure out ways to use large cardboard boxes as houses and forts without ever having seen this use. Alternative thinkers ask, "What could I do with this other than what it was intended for?"

Alternative Thinkers: What Else Could We Do?

The Alternative person's automatic, instinctive reaction to an idea is to think of an alternative to the original idea—that's why we call them Alternatives. What other possibilities are out there? They think *away from* the idea. Say someone suggests buying a new house. The Alternative thinker might say, "Maybe you should think about buying a boat." "Maybe you should buy a business." Or "Maybe you should invest your money in the market." The Alternative person asks, "What *else* could you do?" And the Conventional person thinks, "What are you? Crazy? We're talking about buying a house! Stick to the subject!"

Alternative thinkers also automatically think of nontraditional ways to achieve the stated goal. Andrea and Bob's goal was to provide dinner for and entertain the clients. The Conventional approach would have been a restaurant or home hospitality. Andrea thought of a whole different means to reach that goal.

Laurea, an Alternative thinker, was heartsick when her daughter Michelle joined a cult. Michelle's father, Jim, was a Conventional thinker who wanted to go the usual route of hiring a kidnapper to deprogram Michelle. Jim wanted to use guilt or any other means he could to talk Michelle out of the cult. But Laurea's approach was different: she joined the cult herself. Then, by asking questions that were "innocent" but pointed, she was eventually able to expose the cult to her daughter for what it was. It was impossible for Michelle to rebel against her mom, since her mom was not opposing her—they were in the same cult. Laurea's Alternative way of dealing with a difficult problem proved quite successful. Alternative thinkers start with the goal—what they want to see happen—and then think of unconventional ways to achieve that goal.

Was Queen Isabella an Alternative thinker? If she wasn't,
Columbus had a hard sell.

Don't Be So Quick to Laugh

At Walter's retirement roast, Robert, the company president, made a hilarious speech featuring "Walter's Ten Best Ideas." Everyone roared as Robert went down the list of impossible and wildly funny proposals. Even Walter joined in. Known around the company for his far-out, outrageous ideas, he was used to being considered "the company kook." Then Robert revealed that three of those concepts were actually real ideas the company was in the process of developing. Furthermore, he announced that the company had hired Walter to continue with the organization as a consultant, because occasionally his outrageous ideas turned out to be real gems. The fellow everyone considered the company kook was actually a real asset to the organization.

An Owner's Guide to the Alternative Trait

The Alternative trait is much less common than the Conventional trait, so Alternative ideas may seem ridiculous to the majority (Conventional thinkers). After all, take a look at some of the concepts we most respect today: evolution, a sun-centered solar system, an earth that's round instead of flat. All of these started out as Alternative concepts; all were once regarded as blasphemies. Can you imagine trying to market any of them when they were first proposed?

Alternative thinkers are often ignored, put down, or sent away because their ideas are different. (At least today, they're no longer burned at the stake.) The important thing to remember is that, for an idea to grow, two things are needed. The first is a healthy idea. The second is a receptive environment. Neither one is enough without the other.

If you're an Alternative thinker, you need to position yourself in a receptive environment so you can test your ideas. It's also helpful to find a Conventional person willing to help you work out the feasibility of your proposals to make them more acceptable to the Conventional majority. The world needs your new ideas, and you need to find people who will listen to them and help you figure out how to implement them. Bright ideas can change the world (or at least your small corner of it) only if they have a good audience and a clearly defined means of implementation. Without at least one of those two prerequisites, the world will never know about your ideas, and Conventional people will never be able to play off them and refine them. This would limit the world's creativity!

The Combination That Opens Doors

Conventional people improve on what we already have. Alternative people think of something else instead. Remember when you used to go to the bank and actually talk to a teller—someone who was a real, live person? You sometimes had to arrange the rest of your schedule so you could get there during banking hours. You'd stand in line—always the slowest moving one, of course—and wait until a teller was free. Eventually you'd make it to the head of the line and a teller would help you. Then, voilà, one day some-one invented the automated teller machine. This was a "what-else-could-we-use-besides-a-living-person-teller" idea. It was an Alternative idea. It changed the face of banking. Now we can bank any time of the day or night, with no more running to get to the bank before it closes. The Alternative idea was original and new, and it had a profound effect on society.

Then the Conventional thinkers got their hands on it. As soon as the first bank came out with the new ATM, other banks copied the idea—only they did it better and more creatively. One put a roof over the ATM; another put ATMs in outbuildings; another put them in satellite locations like airports, supermarkets, and casinos. Still another bank improved on the machine itself. The bank with the Alternative thinkers was the first to use the ATM, but the banks with the Conventional thinkers improved upon it.

There are numerous examples of how the Alternative and Conventional traits complement each other. Think about the camcorder and how big and bulky it was when it first came on the market. Soon Conventional thinkers went to work on it, making it smaller and more efficient. Before long it could do more, with much less effort. Look at how Conventional workers have improved the calculator, the automobile, the telephone, the baby bottle—the list goes on and on.

Conventional and Alternative Companies

These traits make their most significant impact at the organizational level. Companies run by Alternative thinkers will do what no company has done before. Companies with R&D departments staffed with Alternative thinkers are the trend-setting companies with leading-edge technology. They develop the new products and are the first in their fields. These are the companies in which people look at the skateboard and think, "What else could we do with this?" And then they create snowboards and waterboards.

Companies run by Conventional people *follow* the trends. If the R&D people are Conventional, the company will be a "piggyback" company, improving on someone else's ideas, products, or technology. Look at how the mobile phone, for example, has evolved.

The Conventional vs. the Alternative Manager

The XYZ Company made and sold products for many years. A profitable company, it became a leader in its industry and held a strong place in the market. Then, suddenly, XYZ found itself with a shrinking bottom line. It wasn't hard to find the cause of the problem: many new competitors had entered the field. Those companies were claiming an increasing share of the market, and that market share was coming from XYZ's.

The CEO was fired and another CEO, Neil, was brought on board to fix the problem. Neil had the Conventional trait, and he reacted with the normal and instinctive behavior for anyone with that trait: he tried to get the company to do what it did in a better

What's the Difference?

	Conventional	Alternative
Responds to stated idea by:	thinking about possibilities, feasibility, practicality	thinking of alternative to entire idea
Gets creativity from:	experiences, outside stimuli	within own mind
Will do:	what's been done, but better. Stress is on fine-tuning	something unique, brand-new, completely novel
Needs:	stimulating environment, facts, concrete information	respectful hearing, help in developing practicality
Shows up in companies that:	tend to piggyback on existing ideas. Need to make products with long-term markets	are cutting edge

and more cost effective way. He got rid of ineffective employees, improved manufacturing systems, made things run more efficiently, hired better salespeople, and in general tightened up the ship. This did have an effect on the bottom line for a short time, and the company produced greater profits.

Slowly, though, the profits started dropping again. What could he do now? He had done all there was to do. He had cut the fat. If he cut away more, bone would have to go—his really good and important people.

Neil was stumped, but XYZ's board of directors came up with a solution. When the profits started to drop, they fired Neil, too, and hired again. With no awareness of traits, they hired another Conventional person who could do very little to improve the situation as the company continued to lose market share. The company shrank to nothing and eventually closed down.

Whoever said, "Ignorance is bliss," didn't know what he was talking about. Ignorance of traits can destroy companies. XYZ needed an Alternative thinker who would investigate new kinds of products, new markets, new uses for existing products, and new market locations (Europe, South America, outer space). If an Alternative thinker had been hired early enough, the company could still have been generating sufficient profits from its traditional business to invest some of them in new ideas.

If you know your company is shrinking, you can take action and get into different ventures before your organization dissolves beneath you. Is your company a shrinking box? Is your industry a shrinking industry? That is what happened to the buggy-whip business. Maybe all those buggy-whip companies started making car parts.

In Short

In both your personal and business lives, an awareness of your traits and the traits of those around you can make the difference between success and failure. When a Conventional thinker finds that what he is doing is not working, he will instinctively try to do it harder, faster, and more frequently. When that still does not work, perhaps he will be willing to try something else. However, the Conventional thinker may not be able to think of something else to try. This is the time to seek out an Alternative person and listen to her ideas. All the suggestions may not be feasible, but they will stimulate thinking and help you to come up with a creative solution to the problem.

If you are an Alternative thinker who's always coming up with new ideas but feels that nothing seems to work out for you, seek a Conventional person to help you develop your ideas and make them both practical and feasible. Any home, relationship, or com-

Conventional and Alternative

Get It in Writing

Have you noticed that many people tend to look up when they are thinking? To find these traits we look up, to the upper loops on the lowercase letters l, h, and b (but not on t's and d's, which are not really
loop letters, and not on f's). People high on the Alternative
trait see all sorts of possibilities. Their upper loops are
wide—at least as wide as their small a's and o's. Those high on the Conventional trait tend to see possibilities only within the narrower range of their
experiences. Their upper loops are narrow or are straight lines.

   A person with a strong Alternative trait—shown in the wide upper
loops—can always think of something else to do.

lead while all about
Here to have
aand individual Sure sold the house

Moderate Alternatives, who can sometimes think of another approach,
have moderate upper loops.

really like living
celebrate the rather than
We'll be delighted to
have regularly brush

Conventional thinkers, who concentrate on refining traditional approaches, have slim or stick upper loops.

much with daughter
CARDIOGRAM REVEALS THE
change I would then   really did buy this card

pany can excel when Alternative and Conventional thinkers are working together, complementing each other's strengths. At that point, the possibilities are endless.

Chapter Seven

Quiet Thinking and Interactive Thinking

Do you really mean it?

ABC'S CHIEF FINANCIAL OFFICER, Grant, a genial man, said to the controller, Erica, "You know, I've been thinking. We're considering acquiring a company in Portugal, and we could really use a report on foreign-operations revenues in the last five years." Erica promptly buried herself in the project for a full week—which meant she had no contact with Grant until a week later, when she

Quiet Thinking and Interactive Thinking
Who Are You?

After each question, circle the answer
that comes closest to describing you.

1. In meetings, I like to
a) brainstorm a lot and bounce ideas around.
b) listen first, waiting to offer a suggestion until I think I know exactly what should be done.
c) talk sometimes and listen sometimes. It all depends on the situation.

2. People take me far too literally when I'm discussing ideas.
a) Often
b) Sometimes
c) Never

3. When I say I'm going to do something,
a) I mean what I say; you can count on that.
b) sometimes I'm ready to do it and sometimes I'm not.
c) I often end up doing something different after I've thought things through more.

4. On the whole, I
a) enjoy meetings and find them a stimulating opportunity to consider more ideas.
b) find meetings are way too long and accomplish way too little.
c) find some meetings worthwhile and others a total waste of time.

5. When I tell someone about my ideas,
a) I have things pretty well worked out and intend to execute those ideas soon.
b) I'm usually thinking aloud and want the other person to act as a sounding board.
c) I'm sometimes thinking out loud and sometimes expecting the other person to act on the idea.

6. People are likely to view me as
a) someone who follows through immediately on ideas I mention.
b) someone who talks about ideas for a while after mentioning them and may or may not actually go ahead with them.
c) someone who sometimes acts right away and sometimes doesn't.

7. When a coworker tells me he is going to quit his job, I
a) believe him.
b) wait till tomorrow and ask if he still feels the same way.
c) assume he just needs to vent.

proudly announced to him, "Here's the report you wanted."

Grant's reaction? "Why did you do that? I didn't want that report."

Erica was flabbergasted. "But you *told* me to do it!" she protested. Grant was certain he had not asked for anything; he was incredulous that Erica would just run off and create a report. He thought she was unbelievably impulsive. Erica was furious and lost all respect for her boss, whom she saw as indecisive and irresponsible.

You've probably experienced something like this with a friend or spouse, if not a coworker. Not surprisingly, miscommunication between Interactive Thinkers and Quiet Thinkers is common— and often costly. In this case, Grant, the CFO, was an Interactive Thinker. Erica, the controller, was a Quiet Thinker. That wouldn't be a problem in itself—except that neither was aware of the existence or influence of these two traits. And since "normal is what I am," each found the other's behavior strange. Not to mention infuriating.

Two months after this incident, when Judi first met them, Erica was still seething. She had decided there was no way to please her boss, and she didn't even want to try anymore. And Grant? He'd concluded that Erica was rash and impulsive, and that he needed to watch her every move. It was only after learning how Quiet Thinking and Interactive Thinking affect behavior that they were able to reconcile.

SCORING					
Add up your total score, using the following values for your answers.			3.	a) 0	b) 3	c) 5
			4.	a) 5	b) 0	c) 3
			5.	a) 0	b) 5	c) 3
1.	a) 5	b) 0	c) 3	6.	a) 0	b) 5	c) 3
2.	a) 5	b) 3	c) 0	7.	a) 0	b) 3	c) 5

A score of 0 through 10 indicates Quiet Thinking. Anyone who scores from 11 through 25 has some of each trait. And those scoring 26 or higher are strong on Interactive Thinking.

Mary, Mary, Quite Contrary, How Do Your Ideas Grow?

While everyone gets ideas, what each person does when that flashbulb first goes off in her head can be very different. It's the processing stage—what happens between the first flash of inspiration and the final, polished idea—that marks the difference between the Quiet Thinker and the Interactive Thinker. Each will develop the idea through feasibility testing, elaboration, refinements, cost-benefit analysis, and so forth. The time involved may even be the

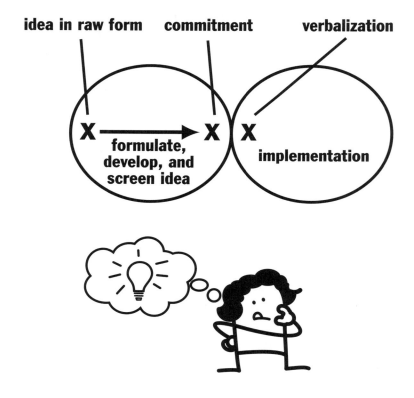

A Quiet Thinker, like Erica, will formulate and process an idea entirely inside her head (quietly); no one else will even hear about it at this stage.

same. And neither type of thinker is smarter or better than the other—but they operate very differently.

People whose coworkers have traits opposite from their own are likely to experience misunderstanding, frustration, and anger. These reactions can be taken to the extreme, and Interactive Thinking and Quiet Thinking traits are major factors in many job loss situations. "Normal is what I am," so in most cases, the person broaching an idea assumes that the coworker hearing it will un-

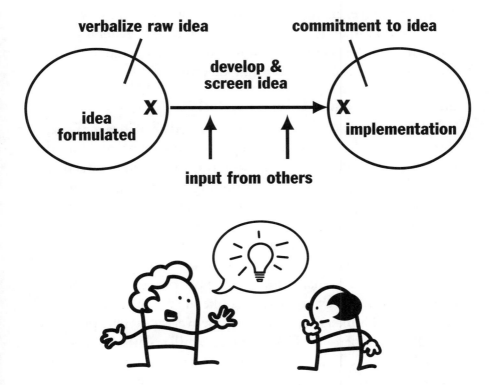

An Interactive Thinker, like Grant, tends to formulate and process an idea through discussion with others. Everybody hears *about it at this stage.*

derstand exactly what he means. That's why Grant expected Erica to understand that he was just thinking about a possibility. And why Erica—assuming that when someone presented an idea, it should be executed—thought Grant wanted her to go ahead. Now.

Oops.

A Quiet Thinker, like Erica, will formulate and process an idea entirely inside her head (quietly); no one else will even hear about it at this stage. An Interactive Thinker, like Grant, tends to formulate and process ideas through discussion with others (or more rarely, through exchanges of letters, memos, or E-mail). When an Interactive Thinker is processing an idea, people generally know about it from the beginning—way before the Interactive Thinker is even sure this is really something he wants to do.

Interactive Thinking: Later, Alligator!

When an Interactive Thinker gets the seed of an idea, he usually throws it out in its raw form: "A report on foreign revenues for the last five years could be useful in deciding on that possible acquisition." From his perspective, mentioning the idea puts it into the developmental phase. What goes unstated is that this is merely the starting point; the idea should not be taken seriously yet.

The hitch, of course, is that listeners can't always tell that; there's no caution light that goes on to tell coworkers that this is an idea in progress. And to make things more confusing, sometimes Interactive Thinkers even say things like "Let's" or "We need to." Some Quiet Thinkers, like Erica, assume every idea that's presented is a fully developed one. Others, more familiar with the approach of the Interactive Thinker (these are often people who are Interactive Thinkers themselves), realize they need more information to know what stage of development the idea is in. Is it still in the processing stage, so they should wait for it to be completed (or help with developing it)? Or is it a finished idea, ready to be acted on?

After mentioning the idea, the Interactive Thinker starts the de-

When Interactive Thinkers first mention their ideas, what they really mean is, "Maybe, possibly, we might, we'll see about doing this if the idea continues to develop nicely."

velopmental phase, during which the idea grows. The Interactive Thinker will analyze the idea, weigh it in the context of his traits and experience, test for feasibility, and so on. During this developmental phase he will allow input from other people in the process of conversation. The developmental phase is, in fact, an interactive process. Those close to the Interactive Thinker will be aware of the idea practically from its conception. Grant thought he was brainstorming with Erica, that they might play with the idea and see where it went, then develop it further, change it, or simply drop it. The one thing he never expected was that Erica would not just play with the idea—she would act on it.

When Interactive Thinkers first mention their ideas, what they really mean is, "Maybe, possibly, we might, we'll see about doing this if the idea continues to develop nicely." They don't usually *voice* those caveats, but that's what they mean.

If an Interactive Thinker gets halfway down the path with an idea and decides he doesn't like it, he simply stops talking about it and starts talking about something else. By the next week Grant had batted the idea around with a number of people, and the process had completely changed his idea of what was needed. He may even have forgotten that he ever mentioned needing such a report.

If Grant had continued to like the idea as he screened it, formulated it, and brought it into final form, then at *that* point he would have been committed to proceeding on it. *Then* he would have been ready for the action phase and would have wanted Erica to get going on the five-year report. Of course, things never got that far—but Grant assumed that Erica would know he was just in the brainstorming stage. Wrong!

Depending on the magnitude of the idea—and depending on what other traits the Interactive Thinker has—the developmental talking phase may take two hours, two months, or even two years before the Interactive Thinker is ready for the action phase. Interactive Thinkers' ideas are like a Polaroid photo that comes out gray and indistinct at first, then turns into a clearer, more brightly colored image as it's exposed to the air. Interactive Thinkers' ideas, like the Polaroid photo, have to get out into the air to become finished. That means an Interactive Thinker has to talk about—or at minimum, write about—an idea to develop it effectively. He may end up rejecting the idea at any point during its development, or he may complete the processing, become committed to the idea, and really want action on it. And by that time, his Quiet Thinking subordinates may be thoroughly confused—not to mention infuriated.

Quiet Thinking: The Implied "Now!"

Quiet Thinkers get unfinished ideas, too, but they don't necessarily tell anyone else about them. When a Quiet Thinker gets an idea, she will screen it for feasibility, elaborate on it, refine it, and analyze it—just like the Interactive Thinker—except that the Quiet

Thinker will complete this process entirely in her own head.

If she gets halfway down the path and doesn't like where the idea is going, she will stop thinking about it and start thinking about something else—and no one will ever know she was thinking about it in the first place.

If she likes the idea after thinking it through, she will finish developing it, still without telling anyone. No one else will have an inkling of what the Quiet Thinker has been considering, because all that brainstorming has been taking place inside one brain: hers. It is only when the idea is fully developed, and she's totally committed to it, that she will mention it to others. And that means that when the Quiet Thinker first voices the idea, she's ready for the implementation phase. She wants—and expects—action. *Now.* When a Quiet Thinker communicates an idea, it's finished and she's committed to it—quite unlike the Interactive Thinker, who first voices the idea not to start implementing it but to start developing it.

Quiet Thinkers say what they mean and mean what they say. The unspoken word that follows the verbalized idea is "now!" When they say, "Let's do this," what they mean is, "Let's do this immediately because this idea is fully developed and ready for action."

Erica was a Quiet Thinker and assumed that "normal is what I am." She assumed that if Grant said something he wanted immediate action—because that's what *she* would have wanted. Had she been around him all week, she would have realized that he was revising his idea all the time he was talking about it (which he did a lot) and changing his mind on the acquisition altogether. Grant had been formulating and was by no means ready for any action, despite his words.

How Quiet Thinkers Perceive Interactive Thinkers

Quiet Thinkers expect others to be ready to act when they voice ideas, and they assume others expect the same of them. Now here's where it gets interesting. Unfinished ideas can be brilliant or they can be stupid. The Quiet Thinker is disappointed if the Interactive Thinker doesn't carry out what seems to be a brilliant unfinished idea. However, the Quiet Thinker is equally worried about the opposite possibility: that the Interactive Thinker might actually carry out an idea that sounds crazy.

The Quiet Thinker's perception of Interactive Thinkers is that they change their minds a lot. They talk about an idea one day and totally drop it for another the next. Interactive Thinkers also are often perceived as unable to make decisions. After all, they may talk about the same idea for what seems like ages. Erica's perception of Grant was that he changed his mind often, never knew what he really wanted, and sent mixed messages. She also thought he was forgetful, irresponsible, and unpredictable.

The Interactive Thinker may talk for months about getting a new job. The Quiet Thinker probably would already have the new job before saying anything to others. Quiet Thinkers often perceive Interactive Thinkers as not following through when "they said they were going to do it" (or as Erica would have explained, when "Grant said he wanted it"). Interactive Thinkers are often seen as being "all smoke and no fire."

However, Interactive Thinkers can also be perceived as team players and good collaborators, because people get to talk about and develop ideas with them. People can see where Interactive Thinkers are coming from and which direction they are going—if they are around for the discussion.

How Interactive Thinkers Perceive Quiet Thinkers

Kate, the CEO of Widgets Are Us, was an Interactive Thinker who used to bounce ideas off everybody in the process of working them out. When she met with Judi, Kate pointed out one of her vice presidents, Rob, and confided, "That Rob is sneaky. He goes and talks to everybody about what he wants to do, then when he's got things entirely worked out, he comes to me and I'm the last to know." That was Kate's perception. Judi explained, however, that Rob was a Quiet Thinker. He worked everything out *by himself* until he was satisfied. When Rob brought an idea to Kate, it was the first time he was mentioning it to anyone. Rob didn't go around working it out with everybody, as Kate did. He worked it out in his head, and Kate was the first to know.

Since Kate was an Interactive Thinker, it is likely that Judi was not the first person with whom she had discussed her perception of Rob—a very dangerous one. Our perceptions of people are based on our assumption that they're doing what we would do. It had never occurred to Kate that Rob could develop an idea to the completion stage without discussing it with others. Kate would have discussed it with anyone who would listen. And of course, "normal is what I am."

Apart from considering Quiet Thinkers sneaky, Interactive Thinkers may also perceive them as being impulsive and shooting from the hip. When the Quiet Thinker says something, she wants to act immediately. The Interactive Thinker says, "Wait! Let's figure this out." After all, if the Interactive Thinker had brought it up, it would have been an idea in progress and not a commitment to action. The Quiet Thinker already has it all figured out and says, "Let's just go do it!"

Quiet Thinkers may also be perceived as not being team players because they don't tell others about their ideas during the development phase. Coworkers or spouses may feel excluded and may conclude that Quiet Thinkers are failing to communicate well. This is especially true if the Quiet Thinker has a strong sense of what to do and how to do it and makes decisions easily.

In the Organization: When People Meet and Minds Don't

Put Quiet Thinkers and Interactive Thinkers together in a meeting and you get very interesting dynamics. Interactive Thinkers get together to throw out ideas (processing them out loud) and to brainstorm. Quiet Thinkers like to do the processing in their heads, so in a meeting they are *taking in* ideas. The Interactive Thinkers talk away, while the Quiet Thinkers sit there saying little. The Interactive Thinkers believe the Quiet Thinkers aren't involved and participating. What the Interactive Thinkers don't see is that the Quiet Thinkers are involved and participating *mentally.*

Halfway through a meeting, the Quiet Thinker will have put it all together and figured out the next steps. At that point, he'll say, "I think we should do this." What he won't say, but will think, is, "Enough talk already. Let's just go do it!" But the Interactive Thinkers will assume this is one more idea to begin processing with the rest, and they'll start talking about it for another hour.

Meanwhile, the Quiet Thinker will decide, "Why bother participating? They don't pay any attention anyway. All they do is talk. Nobody can make a decision. Nobody gets anything done." Because nobody gets anything done *now*, the Quiet Thinker doesn't see meetings as productive. Quiet Thinkers are very impatient to get to the action. They like the kind of meeting in which a plan of action is drawn up and responsibilities are assigned.

The Interactive Thinkers will leave the same meeting saying, "Didn't we come up with some great ideas? We'll talk about it more, then meet back here next week and decide what we're going to do." They will consider the session a productive one. If you have only Interactive Thinkers in your organization, the developmental phase may go on and on because they love to bat ideas around. The nature and length of the developmental phase will be affected by their other traits (whether they are argumentative, have high Autonomy, Internal or External Direction, what type of factors they take into consideration, etc.).

Some people love meetings; others hate them. The Quiet Thinking and Interactive Thinking traits explain a lot about why. Meetings, reporting situations, and relationships are difficult when people with opposite traits are involved. Since "normal is what I am," then anyone who reacts differently must *not* be normal. Or so it would seem. Understanding the differences can lead to the creation of an environment that's more supportive and less critical.

What Quiet Thinkers Need

Quiet Thinkers need to be understood. They may not respond immediately to ideas, but they are taking them in. They need time to think before responding to others, since they do not voice ideas until they are fully committed to them and ready to act on them. In contrast, when they finally do speak, they need people to react quickly and seriously to their statements because they are committed to most of what they say. Remember, when a Quiet Thinker says she is going to doing something—or when she says *you* should do something—she means "now!"

An Owner's Guide to the Quiet Thinking Trait

If you, a Quiet Thinker, live or work with an Interactive Thinker, don't assume that when he tells you something he wants immediate action. Ask, "Is this something you are committed to and you want me to do now?" Find out how far the Interactive Thinker has gotten with developing the idea. Don't take it for granted that people talk the way you do. Especially when the Interactive Thinker is the boss, as Grant was, Quiet Thinking employees scurry into action, just as Erica did. *Clarify.* If Erica had asked if Grant wanted the five-year report now, he would have said, "What? Of course not." But because she assumed he meant, "I want it now," she spent the next five days reporting on those five years.

If you're a Quiet Thinking manager, you need to let your subordinates know about your Quiet Thinking trait. If your subordinates are Interactive Thinkers and you tell them to do something, they think that means, "We're going to talk about it for a while, then decide if we're going to do this." But you, the Quiet Thinking boss, mean, "I want it done now. Put everything else aside." No wonder it's so hard to get people to do what you tell them—it hasn't occurred to them that you really mean it!

What Interactive Thinkers Need

Interactive Thinkers throw around ideas as though they're casting seeds. Some land on rocks and fail to germinate. Others land in shallow soil and grow only a little, then die. Still others, landing in fertile soil, mature and bloom. Interactive Thinkers need a non-judgmental forum—the fertile environment in which they can develop their ideas. Those ideas may sound off the wall at first, because they are underdeveloped. That Polaroid photo didn't look so great when it first came out of the camera either. But if others reject the undeveloped ideas out of hand, the problem won't continue for long—because when the Interactive Thinkers repeatedly experience negative responses, they'll quit talking about their ideas entirely. For Interactive Thinkers, that means the ideas never get developed, or take much longer to develop because they do not get out "into the air." If the picture never came out of the Polaroid camera, how could it develop? When preliminary ideas are dismissed immediately, the Interactive Thinker's creativity is thwarted, and the company loses potentially valuable ideas.

An Owner's Guide to the Interactive Thinking Trait

If you, an Interactive Thinker, live or work with Quiet Thinkers, recognize that when they say something, they mean "now!" So if you have objections you must let them know quickly. You may have to say, "I know you want to do this now, but may I have some time to talk about it with you first?"

If Quiet Thinking Angela says, "We should all pitch in and get Kay a birthday present and cake," Interactive Thinking Aaron must say immediately, "I'm not sure. I need to talk about it a little bit." After discussion, they might realize that no one else has received such treatment and therefore it would not be appropriate. If Interactive

If Quiet Thinking Angela says, "We should all pitch in and get Kay a birthday present and cake," Interactive Thinking Aaron must say immediately, "I'm not sure. I need to talk about it a little bit."

Thinking Aaron says nothing, the next day Angela will present him with a card to sign and will tell Aaron that his donation is $10.

Let others know that you, as an Interactive Thinker, think out loud and do not expect action on everything you say. Tell them when you are not committed to an idea but would like just to run it by them.

If You Have Some of Both Traits

Some people do both Quiet and Interactive Thinking. The good side of this combination is that they're versatile. The bad side is that they can be extremely confusing to the people they're around, who never know if they mean it or not. If they're in Quiet Thinking mode, they mean "do it now"; if they're in Interactive Thinking mode, they mean "possibly" or "maybe we should do it." If this de-

What's the Difference?

	Interactive Thinker	Quiet Thinker
Develops ideas:	through interaction with others	entirely in her head
Communicates:	unfinished ideas	finished ideas
Mentions an idea and means:	maybe, possibly	do it now!
Needs:	nonjudgmental forum	ideas taken seriously
Is perceived by opposite as:	all smoke, no fire; indecisive, changeable	not team player, not participating, not communicating well, impulsive
Can deal with opposite type by:	letting Quiet Thinkers know any objections immediately	finding out Interactive Thinker's stage of idea development; for subordinates who are Interactive Thinkers, make timetables clear

scribes you, it's important to let people know which mode you are in at any given time: "ready to act" or "thinking out loud." Have pity on those you manage—or parent.

In Short

It sure helps to know if you are dealing with a Quiet Thinker or an Interactive Thinker, but since many people are both, it is essential to clarify whether someone really means "now," or "I'm just thinking about this." If you are aware of these traits, you can save time, effort, and grief by asking simple questions: "When do you want this done?" "Do you intend to do this now?"

By the same token, you can prevent a lot of misunderstandings

Get It in Writing

Quiet Thinkers aren't raising their hands to speak all the time; the only time you hear from them is when they are ready for action. Their handwriting doesn't raise its hand, either. Think of the upper extensions on the letters b, h, k, and l (but not d's and t's) as arms waving, wanting to talk. The lower these arms, the stronger the Quiet Thinking; the higher the extensions or loops, the stronger the Interactive Thinking. The width of the loops is irrelevant; it's purely height, relative to the other lowercase letters in the writing, that counts.

Occasionally, we find people who write with a mix of tall and short upper loops or extenders. They are sometimes in Quiet Thinking mode, sometimes Interactive. It's always a good idea to clarify whether someone expects immediate action, but with these folks—who sometimes mean one thing and sometimes another—that's especially important.

Quiet Thinkers don't have much upper extension on the loops of the lowercase b's, h's, k's, and l's.

> STATE OF ONE'S HEART.
> will be very busy on 7/23
> is plan-able or that

Those with mixed traits also have mixed handwriting. Sometimes the upper extensions are on the high side, sometimes low or in between.

> talk about it. Feel free *still difficult for*
> Could you please call *keep rushing ahead.*

Interactive Thinkers make upper extensions that are very noticeable and at least two and a half times the height of their lowercase o's and a's.

> loosing Theirs *Following analysis*
> what you feel he is suited for. *Churchill Heights*

by telling others which mode *you* are in. Tell your subordinates, "I have been doing a lot of thinking about this and would like to have it done now." Or explain that "I have an idea that I want to talk about, but I'm not committed to it. I'm not ready to have anything done with it yet." Either approach can be appropriate; what's important is to make sure others know what you mean—and what you're expecting (or not expecting) from them.

Chapter Eight

The Traits Masquerade

Traits in disguise and in combination

J OY HAD BEEN THE SCHOOL SECRETARY long
enough to see several principals come and go. She knew pretty
much everything there was to know about the school, including plenty that wasn't even part of her job. Then a new
principal, Terrence, came on board. Because Terrence recognized
how valuable her knowledge could be, he looked forward to working
with Joy, assuming that the secretary would be a huge help to him.
But Joy was no joy. Terrence soon learned that he could count on
Joy all right—to disagree with every suggestion he made and to re-

sist every attempt at progress. Terrence felt like firing Joy, but he did not want to let a long-standing employee go. He had to find a way to work with her.

Because he knew about the trait system from a previous job, Terrence decided to look more carefully at what might be causing the conflict. He couldn't figure out, however, whether Joy had high Autonomy, was highly Internally Directed, or was just his personal demon. Then he brought Hedy some of the secretary's beautiful, precise script. It turned out that Joy was only a little above average on Autonomy, and—despite outward appearances—she actually was Externally Directed. The problem wasn't Autonomy or Internal Direction; it was a high Structure trait. Now Terrence knew what was causing Joy's behavior, and he knew how to deal with it.

By now you are probably recognizing many traits in those around you and are learning how to respond to each trait more effectively. This new awareness gives you a powerful tool for managing subordinates, working with difficult bosses, and succeeding as part of a team. Perhaps, like Terrence, you have known traits were involved in certain stressful situations, but have been unable to figure out exactly which ones. Now you are ready to move to the next level of trait awareness, which involves two things: identifying which of several possible traits is behind a certain problematic behavior and recognizing how certain traits (and certain circumstances) can sometimes mask other traits.

Joy, for example, looked as if she were highly Internally Directed, when she really was more Externally Directed. If Terrence had had the opportunity to see Joy outside the school system, it would have been obvious that she couldn't decide between chocolate and vanilla ice cream. However, when someone with a high Structure trait has mastered a system, the system tells the person what to do. Joy knew the system, so as long as she stayed within it, she appeared decisive. She always knew what to do.

In such a limited, familiar context, Joy appeared to be sure of

If Terrence had had the opportunity to see Joy outside the school system, it would have been obvious that she couldn't decide between chocolate and vanilla ice cream.

herself—and had her strongest chance of success. Being high on both External Direction and Structure, she was smart to put herself in a situation in which there was a system she could learn and follow. It made everything quicker and easier, because within the system she knew exactly what to do.

Terrence had been fooled by the context in which he saw Joy, and had limited his thinking to just two traits, neither of which was the real cause of her resistance. He needed to broaden his thoughts about what could be causing the problem. Of course, Terrence didn't know how to find traits in handwriting. If he had, he would have been struck immediately by the high Structure trait shown in her script. You, on the other hand, do know how to find traits in handwriting, so when you aren't sure which trait is at work, go to the writing.

Consider another situation. Jill, who was high on the Pressure trait, could handle pressure and even thrive under it. However, Jill also was high on the Structure trait. She didn't like changes, so if a sudden crisis forced her to change her schedule, it would bother her. She might appear to be rattled by pressure and thus to have a high Non-Pressure trait. But it wasn't pressure that was rattling her; it was change. Once she climbed her mountain of anxiety, she would thrive under the pressure—whereas any person with a true Non-Pressure trait would have found the situation very stressful. The clue is in how the individual performs under pressure, not in how she initially reacts to the changed situation (which happens to be a crisis).

One Size Does Not Fit All

Once you've identified the trait causing the behavior, you can choose an effective method for dealing with that behavior. In Jill's case, if the reluctance to change had been a product of the Autonomy trait, her boss would have needed to allow input or present the change in an unfinished way. Since the behavior resulted instead from the Structure trait, the boss learned to give reasons why the crisis required a change from the usual methods and to allow time for climbing the mountain of anxiety. Then, even with less time to deal with the crisis because she had to climb that mountain first, Jill performed very well under the added pressure.

The Easy-to-Swallow, Fast-Acting Antidote for Misperceptions

You have seen that problem-causing behaviors may not be ill intentioned, but rather are automatic, instinctive, and the direct outgrowth of each individual's unique traits. Often behaviors that initially appear irritating seem far more reasonable when you consider the traits behind them. Instead of focusing on behaviors that may be upsetting because they differ from your own perception of "normal," you can look at the results of the behavior.

That's what worked for Mickey and Lynn. Remember them?

They were the women in Chapter One who shared a belief in using time wisely but who had very different ideas of what that meant. One took a paced approach and the other did her best work under pressure. Both ended up with excellent results, but their methods of getting there were very different because they had different traits. When each focused on the other's behavior, which was very different from her own, her perceptions were very negative. But when they were able to focus instead on the fact that both produced strong results, each saw the other in a much more positive light. Similarly, the college student who crams for exams can get either A's or C's—and so can the student who studies a little at a time for weeks. Their different behaviors don't really matter; it's the results that count.

By now the world should be looking like a nicer place, since you can see that most people truly do try to do the best they can. Few people actually wake up wanting to fail in their lives and cause problems for themselves and others (although some days it may *seem* as if they do).

It can take a while to incorporate this perspective into your thinking, so sometimes it is helpful to keep reminding yourself that each person's behavior is automatic, and that without awareness and assistance, the individual can't help acting as he does. When an Interactive Thinker appears to be changing his mind, for example, he really is throwing out undeveloped ideas. The behavior is still confusing and irritating to Quiet Thinkers, but if you are a Quiet Thinker you will feel better and handle things more effectively if you don't assume that the person *could* be behaving differently. It's as if someone kept making funny expressions while you were trying to give a talk. You might assume the stranger was being rude, which in turn might make you upset. But if you found out that the person had a tic, you would not be offended or blame the individual. It's the same with traits: it's as if people's brains are wired in certain ways.

Still, it's one thing to know that people mean well, and it's something else again to work with them when you really need to get something done. And because different traits can cause similar behaviors, you need to know which trait is operating in order to deal with a particular situation effectively. When the handwriting doesn't confirm the trait you suspect, you can use this chart to figure out what other trait might be operating and—after checking for it in the writing—to determine the best solution.

Strategies for Success

APPARENT PROBLEM: The person seems stubborn, resists change

Trait	What's Really Going On	Strategy
High Autonomy	Needs to put a stamp on each idea	Present ideas as unfinished
Internal Direction	Needs to be philosophically aligned with you	Negotiate
High Structure	Needs time to climb the mountain of anxiety	Give reasons, have patience

APPARENT PROBLEM: The person has a hard time agreeing

Trait	What's Really Going On	Strategy
High Autonomy	Needs to put a stamp on the idea	Present with a red herring, or present idea as unfinished
High Structure	Needs to have the frame narrowed	Be more specific
Low Structure	Needs to have the frame broadened	Allow greater flexibility; broaden the parameters while making sure the goal is clear
Internal Direction	Needs to be philosophically aligned with you	Learn negotiation skills (may not work if your respective goals are too different)

APPARENT PROBLEM: Ideas seem "off the wall"

Trait	What's Really Going On	Strategy
Interactive Thinking	Ideas are not fully developed	Develop the habit of asking if the person is committed yet or if you should wait before proceeding
Alternative Thinking	Idea may seem strange but be useful	Be open to new possibilities, ask how to implement

APPARENT PROBLEM: Lack of follow-through

Trait	What's Really Going On	Strategy
External Direction	Individual doesn't know what to do	Give direction
Low Structure	May have been thinking in broad time frame	Be specific, have consequences for missed deadlines
Interactive Thinking	May not have realized you meant "now"	Deadlines and consequences
Pressure	May be waiting until the last minute to go into uptime	Give a deadline, preferably in advance of the real one
High Autonomy	May be holding up, resenting lack of chance for input	Find a way for person to give input, or set deadline (with consequences for missing)

APPARENT PROBLEM: The person's mind seems to change a lot

Trait	What's Really Going On	Strategy
Interactive Thinking	May have been speaking about ideas to which not yet committed	Give time to process the idea and commit to it
Low Structure	May have been thinking in broader frame; wants flexibility	Put goals in writing and set deadlines
High Autonomy	Didn't feel he was allowed sufficient input or needs attention	Present ideas as unfinished or offer a red herring

Strategies for Success

APPARENT PROBLEM: Person seems to talk too much

Trait	What's Really Going On	Strategy
Interactive Thinking	Needs to process ideas with others to develop them	Have patience or ask for a clarifying memo so ideas will be processed in writing
High Structure	Needs things to be very specific	Provide more information
High Autonomy	Needs attention	Set boundaries; explain the high Autonomy trait; point out the need for staying on schedule

APPARENT PROBLEM: The person seems closed to new ideas

Trait	What's Really Going On	Strategy
High Autonomy	Needs to put a stamp on each new idea	Present ideas as unfinished
High Structure	Needs time to climb the mountain of anxiety	Give reasons for change, have patience
Conventional	Needs to understand how each idea is feasible	Present implementation information

APPARENT PROBLEM: Person seems to waste time

Trait	What's Really Going On	Strategy
Interactive Thinking	Has to talk to process ideas	Set deadlines for decisions
External Direction	Doesn't know what to do	Give direction
Non-Pressure	May be taking necessary breaks	As long as quality and quantity of work are okay, leave alone
Pressure	May be in downtime or may be waiting to go into uptime	Allow for downtime or (if in normal time) give him earlier deadline

More Traits, Same Idea

Of course, there are many more traits in the Piani Trait System than we have covered in this book. But once you understand the basic concept of traits, you have the most important tool: you can recognize that when someone seems to be behaving in a way you find abnormal or inappropriate, it does not necessarily mean that he is ill intentioned. It's far more likely that this person means well but has instincts, based on his traits, that are different from yours. And after all, he thinks that normal behavior is what he would do. Instead of assuming the worst, now you can look at behavior and its results from a different perspective. This alone will improve relationships.

You know that when you feel you are being judged negatively, your defenses go up. Many people use tremendous amounts of energy defending themselves—energy that could be used for more productive endeavors. In both personal and professional relationships, it's amazing what happens when we suspend negative judgments about the way people do things. An understanding of traits allows us, instead, to start viewing each person as doing the best he can with his unique combination of traits in relation to his values. And that approach leads to an increase in positive feelings and a decrease in stress.

Different Values or Different Traits?

We are not saying that everyone has the same values. Values come from people's experiences in life, starting with their upbringing, and may be very complex. In some cultures, acts that would normally be considered criminal are accepted when they are committed against people who are not in the group or family—because those people, being outsiders, are defined as not being human. You don't have to agree with others' values, and you need to protect yourself from those whose values are dangerous to you. There's nothing wrong with assuming the best but locking the door.

However, most of the time the problem is not dangerous values but misunderstood traits and misperceived motivation. Relationships, whether at the office or in personal life, work best when the individuals who are involved share common values—but there's more to it than that. Certainly someone who wants a life of adventure and freedom is not going to be happy with someone who wants a settled situation with ten children; they value different things. However, even if both want a settled life, they can still have many misunderstandings if they aren't aware of traits.

Arthur and Kathleen are now a happily married couple, but their relationship almost didn't survive the courtship phase. Why? Because they had very different Structure traits. Kathleen was very high on Structure, while Arthur was very low on that trait. It didn't take Kathleen long to conclude that Arthur didn't care about her feelings because he didn't call when he told her he would.

Arthur, being low on Structure, would tell Kathleen, "I'll call you after work tonight." Kathleen would, in her high Structure way, try to get him to be specific and would ask what time he'd be calling. If they agreed on seven o'clock, Kathleen would set her schedule for the evening accordingly. At about five minutes of seven she would start hanging around the phone, making sure that none of her siblings tied it up.

But Arthur, in his low Structure way, would come home from work at a different time every night, depending on his workload. "After work" to him meant any time between six and ten. To him, the goal or main understanding was "after work," a wide frame, rather than "seven," the narrow frame of expectation that Kathleen held.

When Arthur didn't call at seven, Kathleen would immediately begin to judge his values ("He doesn't want a committed relationship") and motivation ("He doesn't really care about me"). She judged his behavior as rude and inconsiderate. Kathleen felt unimportant and unloved.

When she complained, Arthur judged her motivation just as

negatively. "She wants to control me," he decided. "She has to have everything exactly the way she wants it." He thought she was uptight and rigid, and he felt both restrained and restricted. It wasn't exactly a recipe for future marital bliss.

After they learned about the difference between Arthur's low Structure trait and Kathleen's high Structure trait, however, these two could choose behaviors to help each other understand their real motives. If Arthur agreed to call at seven and found himself still at work then, he would give Kathleen a quick call to explain that he would phone her later, somewhere between eight and nine. Kathleen could see that he cared and was trying to be considerate, and she could rearrange her schedule. She grew to realize that whenever Arthur committed to a particular time, she needed to consider it as a range of time rather than a specific time.

Knowledge Is Power

Traits are so much a part of the way you see the world that these instinctive, automatic parts of yourself have tremendous power over you unless you learn to recognize them. Once you do this, you gain incredible power.

- You can choose the most effective behavior for a particular situation.
- You can seek out the job and coworkers that will allow you to be most successful.
- You can understand when people might be misperceiving your motives. As a result, you can adjust your behavior or explain your traits and what you need to do your best.
- You can deal more effectively with people who previously would have frustrated you. Now that you recognize automatic trait behaviors, you can assume that these people's intentions are probably good, and can take appropriate action according to the traits involved.
- Instead of assuming negative motivations on the part of others,

you can think about trait differences, look to results rather than methods, and negotiate effectively by considering the traits of all involved.

Psst! Pass It On!

By this point, we hope you have experienced some exciting revelations. When we do trait seminars for businesses, we see people starting to look meaningfully at each other as we describe each trait. By the time we break for coffee, people are eager to talk with each other about their new understanding of what has been going on and why. It's not only more fun, but also more productive if the people you interact with at work and at home understand the system. So we urge you to share this book to get its fullest benefit: more enjoyable and productive relationships. An understanding of each other's traits can be a powerful tool for success for both of you.

And it's even more than that. Knowledge of traits doesn't just give power; it gives a whole new perspective on the world, and a much more pleasant one. We're convinced that this book will not only enable you to be more successful in your work and relationships, but also will help you relax and enjoy it all. It isn't rocket science, but you'll be light years ahead if you try it! ▬

Epilogue

Judi's son Todd died while we were in the process of writing this book. Todd was 26 years old when he died, and he had been sick for a long time. He had not acquired great wealth or fame or invented anything important. He did not die rich by the world's standards, but he did die rich in the love and caring of others.

After his death, his family was amazed to discover how many people had felt their lives deeply touched by him. Many people shared how knowing Todd had changed their view of life.

The most important thing Todd did was to see through behavior to the good intentions and humanity of the person behind the behavior. He did this regardless of social class, ethnicity, religion, or trait differences. He knew how to love and care unconditionally, regardless of the actions or status of the person. His life was a testimony to the value of the approach we have described in this book.

About the Authors

Judith A. Piani, CGA

Judith A. Piani is the president of Piani and Company, a New Hampshire–based firm specializing in personality trait analysis. Through her company she has worked with thousands of executives in client companies ranging from Fortune 100 corporations to law firms and family businesses.

Piani, who has been consulting with corporations since 1976, developed the Piani Trait System to help individuals place themselves in positions that play to their strengths rather than their weaknesses. She uses this unique system to assist organizations with hiring, building teams and integrating new team members, placing individuals in positions that best utilize their talents, improving workplace dynamics, and achieving organizational goals.

Piani earned a B.A. in human growth and development from the University of Massachusetts and is a Certified Graphoanalyst. She has appeared on radio and television, has been quoted in newspaper and magazine articles, and is a sought-after speaker on the use of traits to build more effective working relationships.

Hedy Bookin-Weiner, Ph.D., CGA

Hedy Bookin-Weiner, a Certified Graphoanalyst, earned a B.A. in psychology from the University of Michigan and a Ph.D. in sociology from Harvard University. Formerly an assistant professor at Virginia Commonwealth University, she has published articles in the fields of sociology and criminology. A specialist in genealogical handwriting analysis, she has lectured and published on genealogical and historical graphology. She continues to lecture on a variety of handwriting analysis topics for college classes and professional organizations in the greater Boston area.

Share It With Others

To Order Individual Copies of This Book, call 1-603-465-6193 or visit our web site: www.traitsecrets.com.

To Learn About Lectures, Presentations, and Seminars on the traits in this book, the entire Piani Trait System, or a custom selection of traits for your group, call 1-603-465-6193 or visit our web site: www.traitsecrets.com.

For Information on Placing Bulk Orders, call 1-603-465-6193 or E-mail us at PianiandCo@aol.com.